Political Marketing and the Election of 2020

This book examines the 2020 campaign and election in the United States of America from the perspective of political marketing, always intrinsic to democratic elections. Whether focused on the development of campaign strategy, its implementation via various communication media, or how well that communication resonates and mobilizes the electorate, marketing is central to political campaigning.

The election of 2020 was arguably one of the most unique in recent memory. The campaign took place in a context which included a pandemic that prevented normal campaigning for much of the year, a historically unpopular and polarizing incumbent president and continued adaptation on the part of all political actors and citizens to a rapidly changing communication environment. Chapters in this book, by well-respected scholars in the field, focus on various aspects of this reality. This includes discussion of how candidates use various social media platforms, what effects the social media campaign has on citizens and legacy media, as well as how well marketing efforts resonate with citizens.

Political Marketing and the Election of 2020 will interest students, scholars, and researchers of political marketing, political communication, parties and elections, and American politics. The chapters in this book were originally published in the *Journal of Political Marketing*.

Jody C Baumgartner, Thomas Harriot College of Arts and Sciences Distinguished Professor, teaches political science at East Carolina University (ECU), Greenville, USA. He received his Ph.D. in Political Science from Miami University, Oxford, USA, in 1998, specializing in the study of campaigns and elections. He has been at ECU since 2003. Baumgartner has authored or edited 11 books, numerous journal articles, and book chapters, individually or in collaboration with others, on political humor, the vice presidency, and other subjects.

Bruce I. Newman is a Professor of Marketing and Wicklander Fellow in Business Ethics in the Department of Marketing at the Kellstadt Graduate School of Business at DePaul University, Chicago, USA. Dr. Newman is the author/editor of several books and articles on political marketing, most recently Brand (2018 with Todd P. Newman), *The Marketing Revolution in Politics* (2016), and *The Marketing of the President* (1994). He is the Editor-in-Chief of the Journal of Political Marketing and former Advisor to the Clinton White House in 1995-96.

Political Marketing and the Election of 2020

Edited by
Jody C Baumgartner and Bruce I. Newman

LONDON AND NEW YORK

First published 2023
by Routledge
4 Park Square, Milton Park, Abingdon, Oxon, OX14 4RN

and by Routledge
605 Third Avenue, New York, NY 10158

Routledge is an imprint of the Taylor & Francis Group, an informa business

Introduction, Chapters 1–6 © 2023 Taylor & Francis
Afterword © 2023 Bruce I. Newman and Jody C Baumgartner.

All rights reserved. No part of this book may be reprinted or reproduced or utilised in any form or by any electronic, mechanical, or other means, now known or hereafter invented, including photocopying and recording, or in any information storage or retrieval system, without permission in writing from the publishers.

Trademark notice: Product or corporate names may be trademarks or registered trademarks, and are used only for identification and explanation without intent to infringe.

British Library Cataloguing-in-Publication Data
A catalogue record for this book is available from the British Library

ISBN13: 978-1-032-43471-1 (hbk)
ISBN13: 978-1-032-43473-5 (pbk)
ISBN13: 978-1-003-36748-2 (ebk)

DOI: 10.4324/9781003367482

Typeset in Minion Pro
by codeMantra

Publisher's Note
The publisher accepts responsibility for any inconsistencies that may have arisen during the conversion of this book from journal articles to book chapters, namely the inclusion of journal terminology.

Disclaimer
Every effort has been made to contact copyright holders for their permission to reprint material in this book. The publishers would be grateful to hear from any copyright holder who is not here acknowledged and will undertake to rectify any errors or omissions in future editions of this book.

Contents

	Citation Information	vi
	Notes on Contributors	viii
	Introduction: Political Marketing and the Election of 2020 *Jody C Baumgartner*	1
1	On Political Brands: A Systematic Review of the Literature *Sigge Winther Nielsen*	3
2	A Long Story Short: An Analysis of Instagram Stories during the 2020 Campaigns *Terri L. Towner and Caroline Muñoz*	23
3	Marketing Female Candidates as "Women": Gender and Partisanship's Influence on Issue Discussion on Twitter in 2020 *Heather K. Evans*	37
4	Tipping the Twitter vs. News Media Scale? Conducting a Third Assessment of Intermedia Agenda-Setting Effects during the Presidential Nomination Season *Bethany Anne Conway, Eric Tsetsi, Kate Kenski and Yotam Shmargad*	49
5	An Application of Psychological Reactance Theory to College Student Voter Registration and Mobilization *Tobias Reynolds-Tylus and Dan Schill*	61
6	Candidate Evaluations and Social Media Following during the 2020 Presidential Campaign *Kate Kenski, Dam Hee Kim and S. Mo Jones-Jang*	74
	Afterword: Political Marketing, the 2022 Midterms and Future Campaigns *Bruce I. Newman and Jody C Baumgartner*	86
	Index	91

Citation Information

The following chapters, except for Chapter 1, were originally published in the *Journal of Political Marketing*, volume 21, issue 3–4 (2022). Chapter 1 was originally published in volume 16, issue 2 (2017) of the same journal. When citing this material, please use the original page numbering for each article, as follows:

Chapter 1
On Political Brands: A Systematic Review of the Literature
Sigge Winther Nielsen
Journal of Political Marketing, volume 16, issue 2 (2017) pp. 118–146

Chapter 2
A Long Story Short: An Analysis of Instagram Stories during the 2020 Campaigns
Terri L. Towner and Caroline Muñoz
Journal of Political Marketing, volume 21, issue 3–4 (2022) pp. 221–234

Chapter 3
Marketing Female Candidates as "Women": Gender and Partisanship's Influence on Issue Discussion on Twitter in 2020
Heather K. Evans
Journal of Political Marketing, volume 21, issue 3–4 (2022) pp. 235–246

Chapter 4
Tipping the Twitter vs. News Media Scale? Conducting a Third Assessment of Intermedia Agenda-Setting Effects during the Presidential Nomination Season
Bethany Anne Conway, Eric Tsetsi, Kate Kenski and Yotam Shmargad
Journal of Political Marketing, volume 21, issue 3–4 (2022) pp. 247–258

Chapter 5
An Application of Psychological Reactance Theory to College Student Voter Registration and Mobilization
Tobias Reynolds-Tylus and Dan Schill
Journal of Political Marketing, volume 21, issue 3–4 (2022) pp. 259–271

Chapter 6

Candidate Evaluations and Social Media Following during the 2020 Presidential Campaign
Kate Kenski, Dam Hee Kim and S. Mo Jones-Jang
Journal of Political Marketing, volume 21, issue 3–4 (2022) pp. 272–283

For any permission-related enquiries please visit:
http://www.tandfonline.com/page/help/permissions

Notes on Contributors

Jody C Baumgartner, Department of Political Science, East Carolina University, Greenville, NC, USA.

Bethany Anne Conway, Department of Communication Studies, California Polytechnic State University, San Luis Obispo, CA, USA.

Heather K. Evans, Social Sciences, University of Virginia's College at Wise, Wise, VA, USA.

S. Mo Jones-Jang, Department of Communication, Boston College, Chestnut Hill, MA, USA.

Kate Kenski, Department of Communication, University of Arizona, Tucson, AZ, USA.

Dam Hee Kim, Department of Communication, University of Arizona, Tucson, AZ, USA.

Caroline Muñoz, Cottrell College of Business, University of North Georgia, Gainesville, GA, USA.

Bruce I. Newman, Department of Marketing, DePaul University, Chicago, IL, USA.

Sigge Winther Nielsen, Department of Political Science, Copenhagen University, Denmark.

Tobias Reynolds-Tylus, School of Communication Studies, James Madison University, Harrisonburg, VA, USA.

Dan Schill, School of Communication Studies, James Madison University, Harrisonburg, VA, USA.

Yotam Shmargad, School of Government & Public Policy, College of Social and Behavioral Sciences, University of Arizona, Tucson, AZ, USA.

Terri L. Towner, Department of Political Science, Oakland University, Rochester, MI, USA.

Eric Tsetsi, Department of Communication Science, University of Amsterdam, The Netherlands.

Introduction: Political Marketing and the Election of 2020

The nexus between political marketing, elections, and the Internet is one that is especially complex and interesting. Political marketing has always been intrinsic to democratic politics, and in particular, elections. It could also be argued that the Internet has supplanted television as the primary communication medium in modern electoral politics. Moreover, the Internet now provides a platform and a variety of tools which campaigns make use of to inform strategy. For example, many public opinion polls are now conducted either partially or wholly online, and campaigns routinely use online applications to connect supporters. In short, political marketing, elections, and the Internet are closely interconnected.

While this statement may seem obvious to many, it is clear that it is becoming more true with every passing election. Yesterday's technological innovations quickly become today's standard. Indeed, many of the breakthroughs of the early years of Internet campaigning seem largely passé today. In the 1990s and early 2000s, for example, candidates and their organizations devoted a great deal of time and energy to building and maintaining websites and email lists. Now they understand that the focus of the campaign should actually be on their social media (SM) presence. As another example, campaign advertisements are now produced with SM platforms (Facebook, Twitter, YouTube) in mind. All of these developments have fundamentally affected, and continue to affect, political marketing and electoral campaigns.

Of course on the face of things the Internet campaign of 2020 was fairly similar to that of 2016. The SM landscape was dominated by the same platforms (e.g., Facebook, Twitter, YouTube, Instagram), and candidates, parties and other groups invested a great deal of money and effort into campaigning on these platforms. News organizations, both traditional and new, continued to pivot to the reality and demands of the 24/7 online news cycle. Most Americans were connected to the Internet, if only by their cell phones, and many received some amount of information about politics and public affairs (including presidential campaigns) with these devices.

But this reality is not static. The degree to which citizens, candidates, news organizations adapt to the new campaign landscape (e.g., WWW platforms and interfaces, mobile applications) continues to change. The campaign of 2020 saw continued adaptation to the virtual campaign environment. In addition, the Coronavirus pandemic created special challenges for the campaigns, in many respects testing the limits of how "connected" we are in a virtual environment. The continued changing nature of the relationship between political campaigns and the Internet, and how this affects political marketing and electoral politics is the focus of this issue.

Sigge Winther Nielsen sets the stage in the opening substantive chapter of the volume with a systematic review of the literature on political branding. There is little by way of consensus about this foundational concept that emerge from the numerous studies that examine it, which has obvious implications for research in this area. Taking the various studies into account, the essay proposes a new conceptual scheme and illustrates its utility.

Terri Towner and Caroline Lego Muñoz focus on how both President Trump and Democratic challenger Joe Biden utilized the "Stories" feature of Instagram, which is of course primarily a visual SM platform. Employing a technology affordances lens, their quantitative analysis of Instagram Stories by each in the week prior to and after Election Day shows how each used this feature to communicate and engage with users.

In her chapter, Heather Evans explores the differences in how male and female candidates for the House of Representatives in 2020 marketed themselves on Twitter. Her specific focus is how gender and partisanship intersect to affect which issues are discussed. She finds that even controlling for partisanship, the likelihood that "women's issues" will be discussed on Twitter increases as more women are added to the race.

Bethany Conway and colleagues present research that further explores earlier research on intermedia agenda-setting. They focus on issue agendas during the 2020 nomination season of both candidate and campaign Twitter feeds and the nation's top newspapers. Unlike the balance between the two during the 2012 and 2016 campaigns, where newspapers dominated, they find the relationship between Twitter feeds and newspapers was more even-handed with respect to agenda setting.

In their article, Tobias Reynolds-Tylus and Dan Schill present evidence that both a loss-framed message ("don't be silenced") and a positive norm message ("many college students vote") were associated with greater reactance and diminished intention either to register to vote or to vote on the part of college students. Interestingly, no differences were observed between the positive and negative messages. At minimum, this counterintuitive finding suggests that campaigns and others ought be cognizant of the fact that there may be a backlash effect from positively framed mobilization messages.

In the last study, Kate Kenski, Dam Hee Kim, and Mo Jones-Jang look at the relationship between presidential candidate evaluations and following the candidates on five different SM platforms. Using national survey data, they show that following a candidate on SM tracks with positive evaluations of that candidate, even controlling for gender, age, race, education, party identification, and news media exposure. These relationships are more pronounced among self-identified independents.

Taken together, the research in this issue provides an excellent snapshot of several aspects of how the Internet intersected with political marketing and electoral politics during the 2020 US elections. Even more provocatively, the changing nature of the campaign landscape suggests that each opens the door to further research.

Jody C Baumgartner

On Political Brands: A Systematic Review of the Literature

Sigge Winther Nielsen

The usage of the word brand crops up more frequently in politics. Specifically, in the study of political marketing, a burgeoning set of research has encircled various cases and conceptions. However, the brand concept seeks to harbor a variety of political events, just like a sponge soaking up different kinds of meaning in different kinds of surroundings. This tendency makes it hard to accumulate knowledge because demarcations between various brand perspectives in many cases are implicit, which can impede the clarity and precision in our studies. Against this backdrop, we identify a gap in the political brand literature: a study conducting an overall conceptual inquiry. As such, it is first argued that we need a thorough analysis of the foundation of the political brand concept to uncover the presuppositions underlying the different usages of the concept. Second, we carry out a systematic review of the brand literature on voters and parties. Third, on this ground, we propose a minimal definition and six subclassifications to the political brand concept. Finally, we illustrate the applicability of this conceptual groundwork in order to advance cumulative research in the field.

The usage of the word brand crops up more frequently in politics. Meanwhile, the political brand concept is seemingly encoded with a variety of epistemologies employed in a cacophony of understandings catapulted by consultants, media, parties, and even scholars. This makes the brand concept fairly elusive in many settings (e.g., Stern 2006). Almost naturally the brand concept seeks to harbor a variety of political events, just like a sponge soaking up different kinds of meaning in different kinds of surroundings. Everything can be called a brand. Everything can be explained by a brand (Scammell 2007, p. 177).

However, this proliferation of political brand research comes with certain shortcomings. For example, over time the use, overuse or misuse of the brand concept evaporates its meaning, richness, and applicability. Indeed, some scholars—not all—rarely conceptualize the idea of a political brand and explicate the many diverse subclassifications that implicitly exist. This tendency can be traced in otherwise powerful studies using the term brand in political science, regarding for instance party organizations (Carty 2004, p. 10), party campaigns (Bennett 2003, p. 142), party models (Kirchheimer 1966, p. 192), or party brand names (Tomz and Sniderman 2005, p. 5). Even in the political marketing literature, no foundational analysis has been conducted (for an exemption, see Smith and French 2009 that conducted a review of some parts of the literature on voter learning), although scholars the last decade have examined numerous conceptions and cases.

Of course, the existing contributions are important on their own terms and have provided essential knowledge to the field. It regards, for example, voters' assessments of party brands (French and Smith 2010; Schneider 2004), the influence of party leader brands on voters (Davies and Mian 2010; Guzma´n and Sierra 2009; Needham 2005; Scammell 2007), or ways of creating a valuable party brand (Harris and Lock 2001; Reeves, de Chernatony, and Carrigan 2006). Nevertheless, looking at the field, one is left with the understanding that there is not necessarily a common thread in how these studies fundamentally approach the brand concept. And this in turn makes it difficult to compare and consider the relation between the findings of these studies; in effect sometimes hindering the accumulation of knowledge.

The primary concern is whether knowledge creation has been negatively affected due to the lack of a shared foundation. In other words, the certain way we understand (or do not understand) the political brand concept determines the questions we pose and the findings we achieve. So without an analysis of the foundation of this scientific enterprise we run the risk of *not* producing theory developments or reliable measures, in addition to generalizable and comparable results.

Some degrees of conceptual confusing are apparent in many fields of inquiry. Even so, a more important comfort is that we can approach these challenges if we grasp that the political brand concept does not constitute a unified framework of thought. Rather, it consists of a plethora of conceptions sometimes premised on contradictory truth-claims. The aim of this article is, therefore, to establish greater conceptual clarity by proposing a minimal definition and disaggregating the political brand concept in a number of distinct perspectives. In this light, the political brand concept will hopefully become a more useful construct, which can further advance our knowledge on voters and parties through the lens of brand theory. To reach this goal of encircling the foundation of the field, we seek to combine the insights from the *literature on systematic reviews* (Jalonen 2012; Tranfield, Denyer, and Smart 2003) and the *literature on concept formation* (Baresi and Gerring 2003; Gerring 1999; Sartori 1984). Based on these two building blocks the main findings of this article are a division of the field in six distinct political brand perspectives of the literature, and on this ground, an outline of how to employ these perspectives in strengthening the research program on political brands.

To reach these conclusions we proceed in four parts. First, we highlight the usage of the brand concept in political research and sketch out the challenges by following this trajectory. Second, we create a systematic review of the literature on political brands to establish a pool of articles that constitutes this new field of study. Third, based on these results we draw on the concept formation literature to identify a minimal definition and crystallize six brand perspectives based on an epistemological division. Finally, we summarize our conclusions and discuss the applicability of our findings.

The Usage of the Brand Concept in Political Marketing

The focal point of our study will be authors that employ the brand concept substantially. That is, they engage in a certain brand theory from marketing research and locate the brand as the independent variable in politics. Most of this type of scholarly work can be found in the field of political marketing where various cases and conceptions relating to political brands are investigated in connection to for example brand loyalty (Needham 2006), brand building (Harris and Lock 2001; Reeves et al. 2006), brand performance (Schneider 2004; French and Smith 2010), brand image (Smith 2001; Smith 2005), or brand dilution (White and Chernatony 2002). These contributions have approached the elusive nature of political brands from scratch by adapting and developing a host of valuable models.

The problem this article raises is that the current multifaceted foundation of the political brand concept is not always addressed by the diverse approaches pulling the concept in opposite directions.[1] Therefore, this conceptual dissensus is essential to tackle. In Sartorian language (Sartori 1984), the *intension* of the political brand concept is exhibiting defining attributes that underscore somewhat conflicting perspectives. It follows that actors at the same time in different brand theories are portrayed as cognitive, phenomenological, self-interested, group-centered, socially embedded, or culturally directed. On the other hand, the *extension* of the concept includes nations, parties, nongovernmental organizations (NGOs), interest organizations, leaders, candidates, policies, communication, or rhetoric. The end result is a situation of scholarly diversity—but a diversity that ultimately leads to the political brand term inhibiting multiple understandings.

In this regard, there is a gap in this literature when it comes to an overall conceptual inquiry. As such, it is argued that we need a thorough analysis of the foundation of the political brand concept to uncover the presuppositions underlying the different usages of the concept, instead of only encircling selected parts of the brand corpus. Put differently, scholars have taken close-ups of various brand theories, while little attention has been devoted to taking a systematic satellite photo of the entire field.

To manufacture this photo from above is therefore pivotal. Simply because if we do not take it, this at times confusing situation could lead down a degenerate path in the research program (Lakatos 1970, p. 99; Lakatos and Musgrave 1972) with at least three broad ramifications:

- *Paradigmatic problems*: Scholars will talk past each other and thus do not accumulate knowledge but instead start all over every time a study is conducted.
- *Epistemological problems*: Without a comprehensive mapping of theories, the underlying different intellectual backgrounds of political brands are not explicated. Hence, it is difficult to discriminate between actor assumptions when it comes to making solid theory building and creating theory combination.
- *Measurement problems*: With implicit notions of the political brand concept, it is complicated to determine whether scholars measure what they intend to measure. This implies that it is almost impossible to have competing hypotheses, whereby scholars end up with conflicting claims although believing they measure the same.

We will address this worst case scenario in a systematic review by singling out what has been written about brands related to parties and voters. This fundamental task is necessary in order to provide the conceptual clarity that this article argues is needed. Because when we have identified the articles constituting the field we can unpack the tacit knowledge structures making the political brand research better equipped to be a generative research program (Lakatos 1970, p. 105f).

A Systematic Review of the Political Brand Literature

A systematic literature review is a rigorous, replicable, and transparent methodology for identifying and interpreting previous research relevant to a particular phenomenon of interest (e.g., Cooper 1984; Mulrow 1994; Trandfield et al. 2003). By conducting a systematic literature review this article unwraps the existing literature on political brands, which enables us to provide the desired satellite photo of the field. Through extensive searches and an explicit tracing of the selecting process we aim at minimizing bias and error, while identifying the core contributions to the field of political brands. Overall, a systematic review consists of (1) the definitions of *the inclusion criteria* and (2) the strategy for *locating and selecting studies* for potential inclusion (Alderson, Green, and Higgins 2004).

Inclusion Criteria

Following existing systematic reviews three inclusion criteria were established as guidelines for selecting and evaluating the studies for potential inclusion (e.g., Jalonen 2012). More specifically, to be included in the review a study had to:

1. Be a theoretical, conceptual, or empirical study researching brands in the marketplace of political transactions. By referring to studies that research brands in politics, we wish to clarify that studies merely mentioning the word "brand" without discussing it were not included. Furthermore by focusing on the marketplace of *political* transactions, in contrast to studies addressing the marketplace of *economic* transactions, we narrow our focus to the more or less direct relations between voters and parties=politicians. As such, we knowingly exclude for instance the literature on branding of countries, cities or NGO, brands in international politics, and finally brands in an age of citizen-consumers.
2. Include the keywords "political" and "brand" in its title or abstract.
3. Be published as an article in a peer-review scientific journal.

Locating and Selecting Studies

The literature review was accomplished in three phases (see Figure 1). In the first phase an extensive electronic search was conducted in databases covering business, communication, legal, and social science fields. At a certain point duplicates of articles already identified permeated the result of searches in additional databases (Gerring 1997), and the search was therefore confined to the following seven databases: Emerald, Routledge, JSTOR, ScienceDirect, ProQuest Social Science Journals, Academic Search Complete (EBSCO), and Business Source Complete. The seven chosen databases include a wide range of journals concerned with both the mercantile and the political sphere, whereby a sound foundation for the location of relevant studies was established.[2] A preliminary search without any specific confining criteria conducted on June 6, 2012, located 293,011 studies including the words "political" and "brand." After confining the search to peer-reviewed journals (inclusion criteria #3), the search resulted in the still considerable number of 166,163 articles. The application of this inclusion criterion—peer-reviewed journals—can be questioned. However, the purpose of applying strict inclusion criteria are to base the review on best-quality evidence (Tranfield et al. 2003, p. 215), and though it should not be the quality of the journal but the quality of the studies that determine the inclusion, this was considered a valid balancing of the trade-off between including a large number of studies and conducting thorough and high-quality reviews of fewer studies (Jalonen 2012). Moreover, the fewer journals excluded through the researchers interpretation the more likely it is to reduce risk of bias and errors. To secure that the studies identified were pertinent and constituted a valid but also reasonable population of articles, the search was further specified using Boolean search operators. The Boolean AND operator was used to ensure that both "political" and "brand" appeared in the located articles. The term "political" was deemed important in securing a focus on the political marketplace (cf. inclusion criterion #1) and therefore had to appear in the abstract. The keyword "brand" was specified to appear either in the abstract or title of the journal. The search "political" (abstract) AND "brand" (title=abstract) resulted in 789 potentially relevant articles.

In the second phase the abstracts of these articles were read, and their relevance were evaluated. The majority of the articles in which the key words "brand" and "political" were mentioned were not concerned with the concept of a political brand. In fact, in these articles the word brand was used like any other word: It was neither elaborated nor discussed. Numerous of these articles were also solely concerned with the private sector's marketplace of economic transactions. As such, the word "political" was primarily used when referring to regulation or societal changes related to earning a profit using marketing. In this phase 760 studies were eliminated from the literature review because they failed to meet inclusion criterion #1. Thus, the articles omitted from the review sample through this qualitative analysis were especially concerned with four aspects. It regards (a) brands in terms of consumers' consumption of goods and services (e.g., Micheletti and Stolle 2008; Simon 2011), (b) the political realm as an exogenous force influencing mercantile decisions (e.g., Gru"nhagen, Grove, and Gentry 2003; Kshetri, Williamson, and Schiopu 2007), (c) articles using political terms and concepts as metaphors for elaborating on new developments in marketing or consumer behavior (e.g., Shaw, Newholm, and Dickinson 2006; Brown 2002), and (d) contributions that use the brand phrase in political science without elaborating on the concept and thereby apply the brand concept as equivalent to image, reputation or identity (e.g., Lott 1986).

In the third phase the remaining 29 articles were read in full and subjected to detailed evaluation. In this process eight articles were excluded because it turned out that they neither met inclusion criterion #1. As touched upon earlier there is a fine line between creating an unreasonably large population of articles, which complicates an in-depth evaluation of the articles' relevance and quality, and then specifying the search so that too many relevant articles are left out of the review (Tranfield et al. 2003, p. 215). Using the inclusion criteria too blindly can lead to the latter scenario (Jalonen 2012, p. 7). During the detailed evaluation of the articles it became evident that articles included in the review during the first and second phase contained references to relevant studies that met inclusion criterion

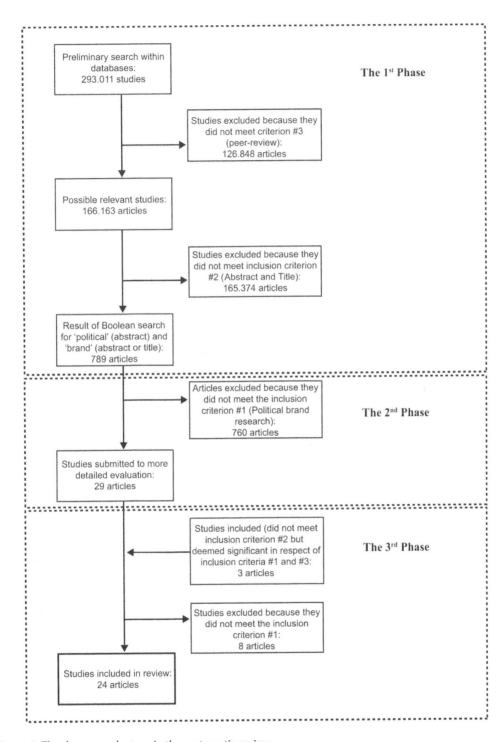

Figure 1 The three search steps in the systematic review.

#1 but did not meet inclusion criteria #2 or #3. Also articles published in journals not covered by the seven accessed databases were considered. Additional studies were therefore located through a snowballing method in which the reference lists of the selected articles were scrutinized for possibly relevant studies (see Hemsley-Brown and Oplatka 2006; Jalonen 2012). This allowed for the inclusion of three studies, which were judged to be important in the light of the present research question.

In sum, the final population was based on 24 articles that can be regarded as core contributions to the field of research on political brands (see Appendix 1). It is probable that studies exist which another researcher would have deemed relevant, despite the employment of the rigorous search strategy. Unfortunately, this is inevitable since the systematic review, though limiting biases and errors, required interpretation that in the end depended on the prior experience of the involved researcher.

Concept Formation: A Minimal Definition and Six Subclassifications

From this departure the literature review gives us a systematic ground, which can be used to properly define and disaggregate the political brand concept. In this regard, we use a template from the literature on concept formation that proposes to look at the conceptual hierarchy between a minimal definition of the concept and the subclassifications embedded in this concept (Adcock and Collier 2001; Baresi and Gerring 2003; Collier and Levitsky 1997; Gerring 2012; Sartori 1984).

A simple picture can illustrate how this hierarchy works. Envision a conceptual pyramid with a minimal definition at the top, encompassing all non-idiosyncratic understandings of the political brand concept. At the next level of the pyramid are located different political brand perspectives, while potential theories embedded in these perspectives are situated at the bottom.

Minimal Definition

A political brand definition can cut through the many different brand interpretations and prevent the concept from becoming an empty vessel. In particular, one way to avoid this pitfall is to present a minimal definition that erases attributes contradicting and excluding each other (Gerring 1997, p. 967). This can be a complex task. Another study[3] identified more than 20 diverse political brand conceptions in this small—but growing—body of literature (Nielsen 2011). Many of these identified conceptions can be considered contradictory or even incommensurable. As an example, a conflict between understanding a brand as stable or unstable is identified (e.g., Hanby 1999).

In that context, a political brand can be framed as *stable*, consisting of a structure of nodal points bound together in the long-term: *"The party brand can produce customer signals that are .. . continuous over long periods of time"* (Smith and French 2009, p. 212); likewise, another scholar supports this assessment: *"Brands are made up of many aspects, which makes them hard .. . to change"* (Lees-Marshment 2009, p. 112). On the other hand, some researchers working with political brands believe that a brand is *unstable*. It follows that a brand regularly alters its position since ".. .*branding is underpinned by the insight that these images are highly vulnerable, constantly changing, and rarely under complete control"* (Scammell 2007, p. 187).

This case is not an outlier. In contrast, we can observe these conflicting attributes in many approaches where the brand is comprehended as both: functional=emotional, individual=social, or voter-driven=manager-driven (Stern 2006). It is beyond the scope and purpose of this article to outline all the differences; this has been done elsewhere (Nielsen 2011). Yet, it should be clear that the field has a diversity of conceptions: a situation of academic multiformity, which is fine in general, but not in particular when we are searching for a common ground to conduct science from.

Based on the systematic review (see all the articles in Appendix 1) we argue that, prima facie, two attributes can act as a common denominator for the field of political brands: "identification" and "differentiation." These two attributes stand out because they do not seemingly contradict or exclude other central attributes proposed by diverging brand conceptions. Accordingly, they seem adequate for the notion of a political brand distilled in a minimal definition:

"A political brand is political representations that are located in a pattern, which can be identified and differentiated from other political representations."

A couple of points regarding the minimal definition are worth elaborating on. The two main attributes in the definition, as mentioned, are identification and differentiation. This implies that when talking about the brand of the British Labour Party, we are referring to whether it is easy to recall the party name and whether it stands out from other "political representations." Further, the use of "political representations," in the definition, can be understood as for example artifacts, names, policies, sentiments, or symbols, which are associated with a political entity such as a party. In this light, the notion of "political representations" is limited to the realm of politics and the particular logics within this realm (e.g., Lock and Harris 1996, p. 14). For example, a symbol is a representation but in order to be a "political representation" different political actors must have employed this symbol.

There has been proposed a wide range of brand definitions over the years; however, what justifies the choice of this definition relates to two aspects. First, it is solely focused on political concerns and not particular business concerns regarding pricing or design packaging, which oftentimes can be located in commercial brand definitions applied in political marketing. See for example Lilleker's (2005) application of Aaker's (1991, p. 2) commercial brand definition. Second, this minimal definition does not side with a particular position in the great debate between considering a brand as "dead" (directed by marketers) or "alive" (directed by consumer; Hanby 1999, p. 7); rather the proposed minimal definition is neutral, meaning it does not engage in this dispute. This neutral position is in contrast to one of the most widely employed definitions in the political brand literature, the American Marketing Associations' brand definition (Bennet 1995), which has been accused of focusing on companies instead of consumers and companies all together.

In summary, we argue that many alternative and competing definitions of the political brand concept would presumably not be universal or they would contradict other influencing attributes. Hence, they are not minimal definitions. However, these contradictions (as, for instance, the above examples of stable=unstable, functional=emotional, or dead=alive) that flourish in some parts of the political brand literature cannot be solved here by a minimal definition, nor should they be. Instead, with the proposed minimal definition, we can move to the next level in the conceptual pyramid. From this position it is possible to encircle the often times contradictory theoretical impulses as subclassifications.

Subclassifications

We have so far established the pool of articles constituting the field of political brands through a systematic review. Further, on this ground, we have, prima facie, arrived at a minimal definition that seems to encompass the contributions located in the review. That being said, we still need to distill subclassifications to the mother concept, which can be understood as more focused perspectives embodying the richness of the political brand concept.

In the concept formation literature it is recommended that researchers look for a relevant dividing principle that can cut up the field (Baresi and Gerring 2003; Gerring 2012; Kurtz 2000). This article proposes to divide the political brand literature according to how scholars implicitly understand the voter. In other words, are the actor assumptions primarily considered rational, emotional, social, or something else? In doing so, the objective is to group the literature on political brands along the lines of various voter assumptions by elucidating different intellectual research traditions embedded in the field (see Figure 2). The technique to develop this categorization is undertaken by first contemplating

	Economic political brand perspective	Relational political brand perspective	Political brand community perspective	Political brand personality perspective	Voter-centric political brand perspective	Cultural political brand perspective
Actor assumptions	The rational voter	The existential voter	The tribal voter	The symbolic voter	The cognitive voter	The cultural voter
Marketer-voter relation	Marketer ⇓ Voter	Marketer ⇓⇑ Voter	Voter ⇔ Voter	Marketer ⇓⇑ Voter	Marketer ⇑ Voter	Society t0 ⇓ Marketer ⇓ Voter ⇓ Society t1
	Active marketer, passive voters who can be manipulated	Voter and marketer engage in a relationship, although the center stage is the use of the brand in the voter's inner reality	Interaction between voters, with the marketer occasionally trying to facilitate	Interchange between marketer and voter in orchestrating the symbolic signification of the voter	Voters own the brand, but the marketer learns about voters and designs ways to change or reinforce their associations	Dialectical relationship between marketer and voter. Voters are drawn toward the party most in tune with popular culture – but in the long-term a new cultural stream can float what is cool or competent
Research tradition	Economy	Phenomenology	Anthropology	Personality psychology	Cognitive psychology	Sociology/cultural studies
Key inspiration in political branding	Harris and Lock 2001	Needham 2005	Phipps et al. 2010	Smith 2009; Guzmán and Sierra 2009	Schneider 2004; French and Smith 2010	Smith and Speed 2011
Key inspiration in commercial marketing	Borden 1964	Fournier 1998	Muniz and O'Guinn 2001	Aaker 1997	Keller 1993	Holt 2002

Figure 2 The six political brand perspectives.

the identified political brand articles from the systematic review and then asking the question: What voter assumptions shape actor perceptions?

Two reasons for this choice stand out. First, the political brand field is composed of many diverse theory traditions and methodologies as the systematic review elucidated (see Appendix 1). Looking at the presuppositions in various contributions, we can reflect this diversity, which is uncommon in other new fields of interdisciplinary study, for instance political psychology (Druckman, Kuklinski, and Sigelman 2009). Second, explicit epistemological differences premised on various research traditions facilitate a fruitful starting point for conceptual clarity in other related fields. For example, we can observe this dividing principle in relation to international politics (Baylis and Smith 2005), foreign policy analysis (Carlsnaes 2002), or institutional theory (Peters 2005).

The epistemological dividing principle leads to the following six subclassifications:

1. Economic political brand perspective
2. Relational political brand perspective
3. Political brand community perspective
4. Political brand personality perspective
5. Voter-centric political brand perspective
6. Cultural political brand perspective

In the following we will briefly describe the six brand perspectives. The main areas of investigation are the different views on (a) actor assumptions, marketer-voter relation, and (c) research tradition.

Economic Political Brand Perspective

This perspective is constituted by rational voters with given preferences, as in theories about micro-economy adapted to marketing research (Borden 1964). Similar to a Downsian approach (Downs 1957), voters optimize utility by choosing the best brand for their needs. The interaction between political brand and voter is transactional and not based on an ongoing relationship. Voters are almost passive and absorb the many bits of information they receive from the political brand (Harris and Lock 2001). The task for brand management is then to influence voters' perception of the brand through linear communication in concrete marketing phases (Niffenegger 1989; Newman 1994). Numerous instruments of spin, television appearances, and marketing tools, such as the 4 P's of marketing (product, place, price, and promotion), will be put in place to make sure the party brand is recalled by voters at the right time and place (Harris and Lock 2001, p. 950).

One example of this brand perspective could be located in the microtargeting literature. Mark Penn (Penn and Zalesne 2007), who directed the Hillary Clinton primary campaign in 2007, underscored the idea of collecting immense amounts of voter data and then segmenting the messages precisely based on the brand image the campaign wanted to convey to certain audiences.

Relational Political Brand Perspective

A relational approach to political branding stands in contrast to the transactional view of the economic perspective (Fournier 1998). The frame of reference is the relationship between the individual voter and the political brand (Needham 2005, p. 349). This perspective draws attention to the way in which voters form different kinds of relationships with political parties, relations that are comparable to human relationships and that are investigated by the individual voter at a very personal level. This understanding is premised on an inner reality that can be based on a voter's life story with a brand ("My father always voted for the party"), rather than primarily using the brand to convey a particular identity to the surrounding world (Scammell 2007, p. 183). The concrete expression of this internal reality unfolds when the voter pictures himself as having a relation to the party brand that resembles a dear friendship, a love affair, or sometimes just a casual acquaintance (Bannon 2005; Needham 2005). Again, the vital component is the individual voter and his or her personal experiences with the brand as a helper in daily life (Lloyd 2006, p. 35f). The actor assumptions are structured around the idea of the voter as an existential being who reflects upon the meaning of the brand in his or her everyday life. This phenomenological perspective instills political managers with an alternative comprehension of how to create brand value (Fournier 1998, p. 344). Fundamentally, brand managers will have to figure out how they can establish "a marriage made in heaven" instead of "a one night stand" between brand and voter (Jackson 2006, p. 149).

As an example, Tony Blair and the UK Labor Party applied this brand perspective in 2005 when they tried to reconnect the prime minister with the British public after the war in Iraq. Labor hired brand consultants who, through diverse qualitative methods, helped to shape a new persona for Blair that was more humble and responsive (see, for example, Lees-Marshment 2009; Scammell 2007, p. 185). The rather bold aim was to renew his relationship based on a long-term commitment of trust with voters that at a very personal level were frustrated with the prime minister.

Political Brand Community Perspective

This perspective examines the brand as a multilateral construct (Muniz and O'Guinn 2001, p. 414). The crucial intersection is between voters themselves engaging in an enthusiastic dialogue on the one hand and the political marketer occasionally trying to facilitate this social consumption of political offerings on the other hand (Tweneboah-Koduah et al. 2010; Phipps, Brace-Govan, and Jevons 2010). Voter assumptions are influenced by the way culture shapes the understanding of a political experience. The outlook is anthropological. In essence, it rests on the discourse of a fan community (van Zoonen 2004, p. 40) or a social tribe (Maffesoli 1992), which constitutes the meaning-making structure through which these voters comprehend politics. This is similar to the dense community feeling that soccer supporters or car lovers can exhibit. As a result, participants' identities are greatly invested in these mostly fluid social networks—and sometimes even in several at the same time (Dermody and Scullion 2001, p. 1089).

To exemplify, the Obama presidential campaign in 2008 employed many marketing techniques to empower brand communities that shared strong emotional links to the Obama brand (Plouffe 2009, p. 77) built on rituals, storytelling, and compassion for other community members. The effect was seemingly profound. Brand community members were willing to donate money, co-create policies and arrange gatherings such as parties, events in galleries, and fund-raising activities (Melber 2010).

Political Brand Personality Perspective

Within this perspective, voters imbue political parties with human personality traits (Davies and Mian 2010; Guzma´n and Sierra 2009; Smith 2009). Some are young, fun, and trendy; others old-fashioned, credible, and hardworking (Aaker 1997, p. 348). The political brand personality perspective emphasizes that voters perceive political parties through human-like characteristics—a process called animism (Gilmore 1919). This logic is premised on personality psychology and underscores that voters can better relate to parties when they can be seen to resemble aspects of voters' own personalities or remind them of celebrities. This mechanism is accentuated when political parties use celebrity endorsements to convey a reassuring and familiar image in the complex world of politics (Chen and Henneberg 2008). In contrast to the relational perspective that underscores the voter's inner reality of politics, voters have to figure out the symbolic benefit of voting for a particular party in order to enhance or augment an expression of the self they wish to display (Street 2003, p. 88). Political marketers then engineer identity packages targeted at certain groups of people, while voters strive to create congruence between their self-image and the symbolic signals various parties distribute (Davies and Mian 2010; Guzma´n and Sierra 2009).

Under David Cameron's leadership, the Conservative Party, for instance, attempted to benefit from this insight. By using an iPod, wearing designer sneakers, and consuming fair-trade products, Cameron suddenly appeared more dynamic through these orchestrated images (Smith 2009, p. 214).

Voter-Centric Political Brand Perspective

Within this perspective, voters are essential to the political brand. They "own" the brand because it is their associations that endow it with meaning (Keller 1993, p. 12). The actor assumptions in the voter-centric political brand perspective are formed by cognitive psychology (Schneider 2004; French and Smith 2010; Smith and French 2011). In this vein, a voter is considered a cognitive miser with no desire to be faced with the huge information costs of crunching policy packages and following the day-to-day news cycle. Voters are just like birds building a nest; they collect bits and pieces of information they encounter in their everyday lives. This information ranges from atmospheres to attitudes, which are stored in their memories (French and Smith 2010; Smith and French 2011). All associations then become located in an associative network that distills the brand meaning for the individual voter (Keller 1993, p. 13). And these knowledge structures—in the minds of voters—can be recalled every time the political brand is stimulated. They simply act as a DNA code for the party, signifying its current status: the momentum of the organization. As a consequence, marketers in this perspective undertake the mission of trying to shape the associations people decide to store in their memories, whereas voters seek to figure out the functional and emotional meanings coupled to various parties (Smith and French 2011, p. 730f).

A host of examples of this perspective can be found. Specifically, we can look at parties that have successfully transformed their brand image; from one election to another, these parties suddenly transmitted a new and relevant outlook. For instance, both the Liberal Party (Denmark) in 2001 and the Moderate Party (Sweden) in 2006 built upon the strategy manual from New Labour's election victory in 1997 that equally changed their brand associations (Lees-Marshment 2009, p. 121, 249). Both parties were now considered vibrant and appealing; people seemingly wanted to be part of the party.

Cultural Political Brand Perspective

This perspective draws attention to the cultural streams in society, especially those streams that are considered cool or competent, which can be employed by people to transmit a certain identity project (Arnould and Thomson 2005; Holt 2002). However, this identity project arises from narratives in society, rather than fragmented associations as suggested by the voter-centric brand perspective or certain personality traits developed in a party's marketing department as proposed by the brand personality perspective. Voter assumptions are thus based on the idea that people are cultural animals that want to figure out what is in sync with the development, and they use this insight as a resource to buttress their life narratives (O'Shaughnessy 2009, p. 68–69; Smith and Speed 2011, p. 1307). Therefore, looking from the viewpoint of party strategists,"... *cultural branding offers the potential for 'Blue Ocean' advantage for the political party that best positions itself to resonate with the zeitgeist (spirit of the age) in society.*" (Smith and Speed 2011, p. 1309). As such, this perspective is fashioned by a sociological reasoning, which considers disruption and disconnection in society to be the main independent variables, instead of the patterns of voters or parties.

One example of the cultural brand perspective can be found in the rise and fall of the British Conservative Party over the last 30 years. By examining the cultural orthodoxies in society over time, it is possible to explain the status of the Conservatives by investigating whether the party was in tune with the zeitgeist. In the case of Margaret Thatcher, a social disruption related to oil price shock and industrial unrest led to a cultural brand innovation by the Conservative Party highlighting self-reliance, entrepreneurs, and small businesses (Smith and Speed 2011, p. 1312). This cultural engineering both resonated with a new stream in society and at the same time was reshaped into the form of Thatcherism.

Conclusion: The Applicability of the Conceptual Findings

Many years ago, the jazz musician Louis Armstrong was asked: "*How would you define jazz?*" Allegedly, in a rather resigned tone, he responded, "*If you have to ask, you will never understand.*" (Un)fortunately, scholars cannot afford the luxury of epitomizing a phenomenon by making references to the metaphysics of the "known unknowns" surrounding a concept. On the contrary, scientists insist on conceptualizing, measuring, and testing the empirical foundation of their concepts. However, the current application of the political brand concept is often more in line with the notion embedded in the Louis Armstrong quote. The brand concept seemingly lacks a general focal point and instead relies on contextual experiences, which consultants, media, parties, and scholars individually project to capture the political realm.

The aim of this article has been to conduct the conceptual groundwork needed to transfer the notion of a political brand from a word to a concept which is amenable to political inquiry. In this regard, we have carried out a systematic review of the literature on political brands related to voters and parties. Next, we proposed a minimal political brand definition encapsulating all non-idiosyncratic understandings from the systematic review; that is, a common ground for scholars to work from. Finally, based on the articles drawn from the review, we outlined six distinct brand perspectives, which can be understood as more focused subclassifications of the mother concept, divided by actor assumptions ranging from foundations in psychology to anthropology.

While this concludes the conceptual groundwork, two tasks remains: first, clarifying how this groundwork can help future studies of political brands and, second, the managerial implications of this article.

Future Studies

We believe that our conceptual groundwork presents three related contributions to future research—contributions that each corresponds to the three concerns, which were delineated in the beginning of the article:

- *Paradigmatic problems*: The conceptual groundwork improves conditions for cumulative research.
- *Epistemological problems*: The conceptual groundwork creates awareness about how to solidly develop and integrate political brand perspectives.
- *Measurement problems*: The conceptual groundwork makes it easier to determine whether scholars measure what they intend to measure, thus enabling a focus on competing hypotheses and contingencies.

Paradigmatic Problems— Road to Cumulative Research

In the beginning of the article, we firstly underscored the risk of paradigmatic problems. It implies that scholars living in isolated brand universes unconsciously "scream" in different directions, which naturally impede the accumulation of knowledge. From this departure, our minimal definition has, prima facie, established a centralized comprehension of what a political brand is.

This minimal definition is nevertheless not enough to address the paradigmatic problems. Today, many articles on political brands try to reinvent the wheel, even though researchers share several of the same basic notions about brands. But here the six distinct brand perspectives outlined in this article can help, since they clarify the broadness of the political brand field; accordingly, scholars can now with this insight state more explicitly which perspective they "scream" out. This is important because if a scholar's brand perspective is not presented very clearly, knowledge will rarely be accumulated. And this is regrettably the situation with some—not all—of the extant research that often treats the brand concept as tacit or eclectic or even develops new constructs resembling existing ones, which ultimately makes scholars embark on idiosyncratic conceptualizations.

More specifically, that is the case, for example, with the otherwise interesting contribution of Tweneboah-Koduah et al. (2010). Instead of exploring one or two existing perspectives and engaging with present research in the political brand field, the authors implicitly conflated different epistemological positions in order to explain the status of the party brands in Ghana. But with our identification of six distinct brand perspectives, Tweneboah-Koduah et al. (2010) could have easily found a stepping stone for their study. The authors might have selected the voter-centric political brand perspective, for instance, and then refined the measurement methods of French and Smith (2010) or even adapted the measure to a context of developing countries. Now, their article is hard to fit within extant research, as it is with other political brand contributions. And that is unfortunate for the study in particular and the field in general.

Epistemological problems—A Firmer Ground for developing and Integrating Political Brand Perspectives

In the beginning of the article, we secondly underlined the risk of running into epistemological problems when doing research on brands in politics. We argued that solid theory building and theory combination would be damaged without clear demarcations between the various intellectual backgrounds surrounding the brand concept. The disaggregation of the brand concept into six perspectives is in this respect an instrument to overcoming this threat since scholars have a background check when they let their actors suddenly switch worldviews. So conceived, if marketers are considered rational and voters are considered emotional, they should remain this way throughout the research unless something else is stated.

More concretely, in various cases, this lack of epistemological discipline has resulted in little theory development in the political brand field. Instead, applications of commercial brand research are abundant, and as a result the field thereby never becomes *sui generis* (something in itself). In this vein, the political brand perspectives in this article can help invigorate an old but common research criterion: *Theory building* takes place *only* within a consistent political brand perspective with one epistemology, whereas *theory combination* between distinct theoretical building blocks can be applied to explain certain empirical phenomena *only* when specifying when=why the epistemological outlook changes (cf., Gerring 2012).

One example might illustrate the argument about theory combination, while it is more difficult to find an example of genuine theory development since little research is conducted in this regard, as noted. In O'Shaughnessy's (2009) skillful expose' of the so-called "Nazi brand," he engaged with at least three distinct brand perspectives based on intellectual traditions from economics, personality psychology, and sociology. In such a study it is natural to investigate and integrate these perspectives; however, he never clearly states the dissimilarities of these three drivers of the "Nazi brand." As a consequence, O'Shaughnessy (2009) illuminates the functioning of a political brand at a general level, while neglecting how the interplay of these very different understandings of the brand comes together and explain the outcome of the "Nazi brand."

Measurement Problems—Enabling a focus on Competing Hypotheses and Contingencies

In the beginning of the article, we thirdly emphasized the risk of measurement problems stemming from implicit notions of the brand concept. That is, measurement validity is threatened when it is difficult to discern whether scholars measure what they intend to measure. As it is today, some scientists outline conclusions, which highlight quite different effects of brands; despite our thinking that we are elaborating on the same concept, we in fact measure different tacit brand perspectives. Here, conceptual clarity will make sure that we do not mesh empirically distinct phenomena.

For instance, Harris and Lock (2001) present a somewhat generic understanding of a political brand, whereas at another extreme, TweneboahKoduah et al. (2010) delineate an overlapping understanding of a political brand almost spanning all six brand perspectives. So, the question then arises: Are the measured brands in these two studies comparable? The answer must be: not quite. While they both utilize the brand concept as an explanatory variable, they choose widely different empirical indicants. The basic point is that few studies are comparable in extant political brand literature. In reality, no studies so far have outlined competing hypotheses with different brand perspectives battling each other to grasp the contingencies of these approaches (for a related critique see Henneberg 2008, p. 153f).

Managerial Implications

The conceptual groundwork of this article might seem like a scholastic exercise removed from the political marketing agency. It is not necessarily so, however. Practitioners depend on clear brand instruments, which they know when and where to apply. The implication for political marketers of this study is therefore dual.

First, the six brand perspectives derived from the systematic literature review are feasible tool kits for marketers that need a summary of the existing theoretical and methodological strands. Although more field research bridging theory and practice is needed, we do have examples from Tony Blair's "make-over to a humble man trying to reconnect with voters" in 2005, where his advisors deliberately changed from subscribing to a voter-centric brand perspective to engaging with a relational brand perspective (Scammell 2007, p. 185). And this clarity in thought can help brand managers to strategize at a more sophisticated level.

Second, the six brand perspectives can take practitioners through one important step: outlining the universe of brand instruments and methods, as just highlighted. Nonetheless, these brand perspectives do not enable a political marketer to conduct cogent decisions about which perspective to leverage in a particular situation. Here, practitioners must await motion from the scholarly community to obtain knowledge describing the contingencies of the various perspectives, as this paper suggests future research should do. That said, brand managers can already now look at case studies, outlined as small examples in this article when we described the six perspectives, in addition to consult existing studies explaining the potency of various marketing instruments in different electoral settings (e.g., Dean 2004, p. 149). In this fashion, practitioners will sense that, for example, the relational brand perspective seems to be most suitable between elections and the economic brand perspective might be best to leverage during a campaign, whereas the cultural brand perspective probably should be employed to develop a long-term strategy over several elections.

Notes

1. A couple of exemptions are relevant to mention. For example, Smith and French (2009, p. 214f) underscore different intellectual backgrounds related to a host of models they ascribe to the voter-centric perspective (i.e., named a consumer perspective). Also, Smith and Speed (2011, p. 1307) situate their cultural brand model within other implicit research traditions that they label "economics" and "psychology." Finally, Needham (2005, p. 345) explicates how her relational perspective is different from a transactional approach; meanwhile she consciously ends up with a model that blends all kinds of instrument drawn from various epistemological positions. Overall, some authors refer to different strands in the political brand literature, but few take the consequences of these differences, as we shall explore in this paper.
2. The wide-ranging database Web of Science might have been preferable to search in instead of looking at diverse databases. However, after searching in Web of Science, it was evident that most of the journals publishing research on political brands were not included. In this light we followed other systematic reviews that encircle relevant databases (see Hemsley-Brown and Oplatka 2006; Jalonen 2012).
3. It is important to note that the development of this definition (and its relation to other definitions) has been outlined in a book chapter on brand definitions (Nielsen 2011). Using Gerring's (1997, p. 967) "comprehensive framework," the whole semantic field regarding the political brand was unpacked in this chapter to illuminate contradictions and search for attributes that unite the field in a minimal definition (we understand an attribute as a central characteristic in a certain author's brand conception).

References

Aaker, D. A. (1991). *Managing brand equity: Capitalizing on the value of a brand name.* New York: The Free Press.

Aaker, J. L. (1997). Dimensions of brand personality. *Journal of Marketing Research, 34*(3), 347–356.

Adcock, R., and D. Collier. (2001). Measurement validity: A shared standard for qualitative and quantitative research. *American Political Science Review, 95*(3), 529–546.

Alderson, P., S. Green, and J. P. T. Higgins (Eds.) (2004). *Cochrane reviewers' handbook* 4.2.2. [updated March 2004], Cochrane Library, Issue 1. Chichester, UK: John Wiley and Sons.

Arnould, E. J., and C. J. Thompson. (2005). Consumer culture theory (CCT): Twenty years of research. *Journal of Consumer Research, 31*(4), 868–882.

Bannon, D. (2005). Relationship marketing and the political process. *Journal of Political Marketing, 4*(2–3), 73–90.

Baresi, P. A., and J. Gerring. (2003). Putting ordinary language to work: A min-max strategy of concept formation in social sciences. *Journal of Theoretical Politics, 15*(2), 201–232.

Baylis, J., and S. Smith (Eds.). (2005). *The globalization of world politics, an introduction to international relations* (3rd ed.). Oxford: Oxford University Press.

Bennet, P. D. (1995). *Dictionary of marketing terms* (2nd ed.). Chicago: American Marketing Association.

Bennett, L. W. (2003). Lifestyle politics and citizen-consumers. In *Media and the restyling of politics*, J. Corner and D. Pels ed. London: Sage.

Borden, N. H. (1964). The concept of the marketing mix. In *Science in marketing*, George Schwartz ed. New York: Wiley.

Brown, S. (2002). Vote, vote, vote for Philip Kotler. *European Journal of Marketing, 36*(3), 313–324.

Carty, K. R. (2004). Parties as franchise systems: The stratarchical organizational imperative. *Party Politics, 10*(1), 5–24.

Carlsnaes, W. (2002). On the study of foreign policy. In *Handbook of international relations*, ed. W. Carlsnaes, T. Risse, and B. A. Simmons. London: Sage.

Chen, Y., and S. C. Henneberg. (2008). Celebrity political endorsment. *Journal of Political Marketing, 6*(4), 1–31.

Collier, D., and S. Levitsky. (1997). Democracy with adjectives: Conceptual innovation in comparative research. *World Politics, 49*(3), 430–451.

Cooper, H. M. (1984). *The integrative research review: A systematic approach*. Beverly Hills, CA: Sage Publications.

Davies, G., and T. Mian. (2010). The reputation of the party leader and of the party being led. *European Journal of Marketing, 44*(3=4), 331–350.

Dean, D. (2004). Political research and practitioner approaches: A review of the research methods used in voting behaviour research. *Journal of Public Affairs, 4*(2), 145–154.

Dermody, J., and R. Scullion. (2001). Delusions or grandeur? Marketing's contribution to "meaningful" Western political consumption. *European Journal of Marketing, 35*(9–10), 1085–1098.

Downs, A. (1957). *An economic theory of democracy*. New York: Harper & Brothers.

Druckman J. N., J. H. Kuklinski, and L. Sigelman. (2009). The unmet potential of interdisciplinary research. *Political Behavior, 31*(4), 485–510.

Fournier, S. (1998). Consumer and their brands: developing relationship theory in consumer research. *Journal of Consumer Research, 24*(4), 343–373.

French, A., and G. Smith. (2010). Measuring political brand equity: A consumer oriented approach. *European Journal of Marketing, 44*(3=4), 460–477.

Gerring, J. (1997). Ideology: A definitional analysis. *Political Research Quarterly, 50*(4), 957–994.

Gerring, J. (1999). What makes a concept good? A criterial framework for understanding concept formation in the social sciences. *Polity, 31*(3), 357–393.

Gerring, J. (2012). *Social science methodology: A unified framework*. New York: Cambridge University Press.

Gilmore, G. W. (1919). *Animism: Or thought currents of primative peoples*. Boston: Marshall Jones Company.

Gru¨nhagen, M., S. J. Grove, and J. W. Gentry. (2003). The dynamics of store hour changes and consumption behavior: Results of a longitudinal study of consumer attitudes toward Saturday shopping in Germany. *European Journal of Marketing, 37*(11=12), 1801–1817.

Guzma´n, F., and V. Sierra. (2009). A political candidate's brand image scale: Are political candidates brands? *Journal of Brand Management, 17*(3), 207–217.

Hanby, T. (1999). Brands—dead or alive? *Journal of the Market Research Society, 41*(1), 7–18.

Harris, P., and A. Lock. (2001). Establishing the Charles Kennedy brand: A strategy for an election the result of which is a foregone conclusion. *Journal of Marketing Management, 17*(9=10), 943–956.

Hemsley-Brown, J. V., and I. Oplatka. (2006). Universities in a competitive global marketplace: A systematic review of the literature on higher education marketing. *International Journal of Public Sector Management, 19*(4), 316–338.

Henneberg, S. (2008). An epistemological perspective on research in political marketing. *Journal of Political Marketing, 7*(2), 151–182.

Hoegg, J., and M. V. Lewis. (2011). The impact of candidate appearance and advertising strategies on election results. *Journal of Marketing Research, 48*(5), 895–909.

Holt, D. B. (2002). Why do brands cause trouble? A dialectical theory of consumer culture and branding. *Journal of Consumer Research, 29*, 70–90.

Jackson, N. (2006). Political parties, their e-newsletters and subscribers: One night stands or a marriage made in heaven? In P. Davies, and B. Newman (Ed.), *Winning elections with political marketing*. New York: The Haworth Press.

Jalonen, H. (2012). The uncertainty of innovation: A systematic review of the literature. *Journal of Management Research*, *4*(1), 1–47.

Keller, K. L. (1993). Conceptualizing, measuring and managing customer-based brand equity. *Journal of Marketing*, *57*(1), 1–22.

Kirchheimer, O. (1966). The transformation of the Western European party systems. In J. LaPalombara and M. Weiner (Ed.), *Political parties and political development*, Princeton: Princeton University Press.

Kshetri, N., N. C. Williamson, and A. Schiopu. (2007). Economics and politics of advertising: Evidence from the enlarging European Union. *European Journal of Marketing*, *41*(3=4), 349–366.

Kurtz, M. (2000). Understanding peasant revolution: From concept to theory and case. *Theory and Society*, *29*(1), 93–124.

Lakatos, I. (1970). History of science and its rational reconstructions, *PSA: Proceedings of the Biennial Meeting of the Philosophy of Science Association*, *1970*, 91–136.

Lakatos, I., and A. Musgrave. (1972). *Criticism and the growth of knowledge*. London: Cambridge University Press.

Lees-Marshment, J. (2009). *Political marketing, principles and applications*. London: Routledge.

Lilleker, D. G. (2005). The impact of political marketing on internal party democracy. *Parliamentary Affairs*, *58*(3), 570–584.

Lloyd, J. (2006). *Brand conceptualisation*. PhD dissertation. Bristol: University of the West of England.

Lock, A., and P. Harris. (1996). Political marketing—vive la diffe'rence!, *European Journal of Marketing*, *30*(10), 14–24.

Lott Jr., J. R. (1986). Brand names and barriers to entry in political markets. *Public Choice*, *51*(1), 87–92.

Maffesoli, M. (1992). *La transfiguration du politique, la tribalisation du monde*. Paris: Bernard Grasset.

Marsh, D., and P. Fawcett. (2011). Branding, politics and democracy. *Policy Studies*, *32*(5), 515–530.

Mart'ın-Barbero, S. (2006). Web recommunication: The political brand identity conceptual approach. *Corporate Reputation Review*, *8*(4), 339–348.

Melber, A. (2010). *Year one of organizing for America: The permanent field campaign in a digital age*. http://ssrn.com/abstract=1536351

Micheletti, M., and D. Stolle. (2008). Fashioning social justice through political consumerism, capitalism, and the Internet. *Cultural Studies*, *22*(5), 749–769.

Mulrow, C. D. (1994). Systematic reviews: Rationale for systematic reviews. *British Medical Journal*, *309*(6954), 597–599.

Muniz, A. M., and T. C. O'Guinn. (2001). Brand community. *Journal of Consumer Research*, *27*(4), 412–432.

Needham, C. (2005). Brand leaders: Clinton, Blair, and the limitations of the permanent campaign. *Political Studies*, *53*(2), 343–361.

Needham, C. (2006). Brands and political loyalty. *Journal of Brand Management*, *13*(3), 178–187.

Newman, B. (1994). *The marketing of the president*. Thousand Oaks, CA: Sage.

Nielsen, S. W. (2011). '*Om Politiske Brands' in Politisk Marketing Personer, Partier & Praksis*. Karnov Group: Copenhagen.

Niffenegger, P. B. (1989). Strategies for success from the political marketers. *Journal of Consumer Marketing*, *6*(1), 45–54.

O'Cass, A., and R. Voola. (2011). Explications of political market orientation and political brand orientation using the resource-based view of the political party. *Journal of Marketing Management*, *27*(5=6), 627–645.

O'Shaughnessy, N. (2009). Selling Hitler: Propaganda and the Nazi brand. *Journal of Public Affairs*, *9*(1), 55–76.

Penn, M., and K. Zalesne. (2007). *Microtrends: The small forces behind tomorrow's big changes*. New York: Twelve.

Peters, B. G. (2005). *Institutional theory in political science, the »new« institutionalism*. London: Continuum.

Phipps, M., J. Brace-Govan, and C. Jevons. (2010). The duality of political brand equity. *European Journal of Marketing*, *44*(3=4), 496–514.

Plouffe, D. (2009). *The audicity to win*. Penguin Books: New York.

Raphael, T. (2009). The body electric: GE, TV, and the Reagan brand. *TDR (1988–)*, *53*(2), 113–138.

Reeves, P., L. de Chernatony, and M. Carrigan. (2006). Building a political brand: Ideology or voter-driven strategy. *Journal of Brand Management*, *13*(6), 418–428.

Sartori, G. (1984). *Social science concepts, a systematic analysis*. Beverly Hills: Sage. Scammell, M. (2007). Political brands and consumer citizens: The rebranding of Tony Blair, *Annals of the American Academy of Political and Social Science*, *611*, 176–192.

Schneider, H. (2004). Branding in politics—Manifestations, relevance and identityoriented management. *Journal of Political Marketing*, *3*(3), 41–67.

Shaw, D., T. Newholm, and R. Dickinson. (2006). Consumption as voting: An exploration of consumer empowerment. *European Journal of Marketing*, *40*(9=10), 1049–1067.

Simon, B. (2011). Not going to Starbucks: Boycotts and the out-sourcing of politics in the branded world. *Journal of Consumer Culture, 11*(2), 145–167.

Smith, G. (2001). The 2001 general election: Factors influencing the brand image of political parties and their leaders. *Journal of Marketing Management, 17*(9=10), 989–1006.

Smith, G. (2005). Politically significant events and their effect on the image of political parties. *Journal of Political Marketing, 4*(2–3), 91–114.

Smith, G. (2009). Conceptualizing and testing brand personality in British politics. *Journal of Political Marketing, 8*(3), 209–232.

Smith, G., and A. French. (2009). The political brand: A consumer perspective. *Marketing Theory, 9*(2), 209–226.

Smith, G., and A. French. (2011). Measuring the changes to leader brand associations during the 2010 election campaign. *Journal of Marketing Management, 27*(7=8), 721–738. Smith, G., and R. Speed. (2011). Cultural branding and political marketing: An exploratory analysis. *Journal of Marketing Management, 27*(13=14), 1304–1321.

Stern, B. (2006). What does brand mean? Historical-analysis method and construct definition. *Journal of the Academy of Marketing Science, 34*(2), 216–223.

Street, J. (2003). The celebrity politician: Political style and popular culture. In J. Corner and D. Pels (Ed.), *Media and the restyling of politics.* 85–99. Thousand Oaks, CA: Sage.

Tomz, M., and P. M. Sniderman. (2005). *Brand names and the organization of mass belief systems.* Paper presented at the Annual Meeting of the Midwest Political Association, Chicago.

Tranfield, D., D. Denyer, and P. Smart. (2003). Towards a methodology for developing evidence-informed management knowledge by means of systematic review. *British Journal of Management, 14*(3), 207–222.

Tweneboah-Koduah, E. Y., M. Akotia, C. S. Akotia, and R. Hinson. (2010). Political party brand and consumer choice in Ghana. *Journal of Management Policy & Practice, 11*(5), 79–88.

van Zoonen, L. (2004). Imagining fan democracy. *European Journal of Communication, 19*(1), 39–52.

White, J., and L. de Chernatony. (2002). New labour: A study of the creation, development, and demise of a political brand. *Journal of Political Marketing, 1*(2–3), 45–52.

APPENDIX A. Articles from the Systematic Literature Review

The appendix lists the selected articles in alphabetical order along with purpose of the study, theoretical framework, methodology, and the subclassification(s) the particular article is premised on. These subclassifications are discussed in detail in the main text.

The appendix presents a rich amount of data that we do not elaborate on in this article. However, future studies might well explore patterns in the political brand field in terms of origin of authors, countries studied, which methodologies that are most prevalent, etc.

Article	Purpose of the study	Theoretical framework	Methodology	Brand subclassification
				1. Economic political brand perspective 2. Relational political brand perspective 3. Political brand community perspective 4. Political brand personality perspective 5. Voter-centric political brand perspective 6. Cultural political brand perspective
Davies & Mian (2010)	To analyze the similarity of the reputation of political leaders with those of their parties and to assess the claim of causal links. The research is conducted with data from two UK general elections.	Multidimensional measure of brand personality.	Two surveys each prior to UK general elections in 2001 and 2005.	4
French & Smith (2010)	To explore and measure voters' perceptions of a party's political brand in the UK.	Applying Keller's (1993) consumer-oriented / voter-centric approach to performing associative brand maps.	Small-scale convenient sample of around 150 undergraduates.	5
Guzmán & Sierra (2009)	To analyze and develop a measure for political candidate's brand image in Mexico's 2006 election.	Brand image framework constructed from a combination of two established measures of brand personality and candidate personality.	Survey; model construction; conceptual analysis.	4
Harris & Lock (2001)	To analyze the branding of a party leader through the case of the Liberal Democrats in the UK 2001 general election.	Political marketing; political branding; party positioning.	Case study: Descriptive analysis	1, 4
Hoegg & Lewis (2011)	To analyze how candidate appearance interacts with political party brand image, advertising spending, and negative advertising in the United States.	Political marketing; political branding; party positioning; visual inferences.	Laboratory study	4

Marsh & Fawcett (2011)	To analyze the relationship between branding and politics world wide and its implications for democracy.	Political branding; governance and democracy.	Conceptual analysis	1, 2, 3, 5
Marti'n-Barbero (2006)	To analyze strategic political communication and the manifestation of brand identity on political candidate's and parties' websites.	Political communication; Political marketing; Brand Identity Web Analysis Method (BIWAM); Political Communication Web Identity Active Content System (PCWIACS).	Content analysis	1, 4, 5
Needham (2005)	To assess incumbent's strategies for establishing a post-election relationship with voters in the case of Blair in the UK and Clinton in the U.S.	Relationship marketing; political branding.	Conceptual analysis, model construction, and explorative case studies	1, 2, 4
Needham (2006)	To analyze in general how parties develop brand attributes in their leaders to maintain relationships with voters beyond the initial transaction.	Political marketing; relationship marketing; brand loyalty.	Conceptual analysis	2
O'Cass & Voola (2011)	To explicate the concepts of political marketing orientation and political brand orientation.	Resource-based view of the firm applied on the party brands.	Conceptual analysis	1
O'Shaughnessy (2009)	To analyze how Nazism in Germany functioned as a brand.	Political branding strategies.	Single case study	1, 4, 6
Phipps, Brace-Govan, & Jevons (2010)	To examine consumer contribution to political brands and how political consumers affect the politician's brand equity in Australia.	Applying Aaker's (1997) "Brand Equity Ten."	Comparative case study with two contrasting cases	4
Raphael (2009)	To analyze the creation of the Ronald Reagan brand in United States.	Brand loyalty: Strategic, political communication and politics from a theatrical / show business outlook.	Single case study	1, 4, 6
Reeves, Chernatony, & Carrigan (2006)	To demonstrate in general how it is increasingly meaningful to apply the principles of brand management to political parties and to discuss the implications of this.	Political brand marketing.	Conceptual analysis	1, 2, 3

(Continued)

Article	Purpose of the study	Theoretical framework	Methodology	Brand subclassification
Scammell (2007)	To examine how the brand concept is used in politics and how branding has become the new hallmark for marketed parties in the Western world.	Political branding, relational branding; political marketing.	Conceptual analysis	2
Schneider (2004)	To develop a method for measuring and evaluating brand status. The case is Germany.	Identity-Oriented brand management; applying and adapting Keller's (1993) brand theory complex.	Survey of parties and party leaders. Model construction	5
Smith (2001)	To examine factors influencing the political brand images drawing on the case of the 2001 UK general election.	Political brand image management.	Single case study	1
Smith (2005)	To ascertain how politically significant events affect party brand image. The case is UK politics in the era of New Labour.	Eclectic approach combining marketing, branding and consumer behavior literature.	Conceptual model construction and critical case study	1
Smith (2009)	To develop a conceptual model for measuring political brand personality in the UK.	Employing and adapting Aaker's (1997) brand personality scale.	Conceptual analysis Model construction Small-scale convenient sample Factor analysis	4
Smith & French (2009)	To justify and theoretically support seeing political parties as brands and to ascertain how political brand images are stored in consumer memory.	Consumer-based cognitive learning approaches.	Review and conceptual analysis	1, 2, 3, 4, 5
Smith & French (2011)	To measure and analyze changes to voters' perceptions of the leader brands during the UK 2010 general election.	Applying Keller's (1993) consumer-oriented / voter-centric approach to performing associative brand maps.	Small-scale convenient sample of around 150 undergraduates	5
Smith & Speed (2011)	To explore the usefulness of analyzing political brands as cultural brands. A historical overview of the Conservative Party in the UK.	Consumer brand culture theory applied to politics.	Conceptual analysis; longitudinal single case study	6
Tweneboah-Koduah, Yaw, Akotia, Akotia, & Hinson (2010)	To analyze political parties' brand management. In particular, the perceptions of party brands among voters in Ghana's developing economy.	Employing different political brand management theories.	Conceptual analysis; 82 focus group interviews and 120 in-depth interviews	1,2,3,4,5
White & Chernatony (2002)	To examine political parties' use of branding by assessing the case of New Labour.	Branding and political communication.	Single case study	1, 3, 5, 6

A Long Story Short: An Analysis of Instagram Stories during the 2020 Campaigns

Terri L. Towner and Caroline Muñoz

ABSTRACT
Political campaigns are becoming immensely visual, with many platforms, such as YouTube, Instagram, and SnapChat, employed by candidates. We focus on the second most popular platform, Instagram, examining how the 2020 presidential candidates, Donald Trump and Joe Biden, utilize "Stories" in their digital campaigns. Instagram "Stories" allow users to capture and post related images and videos in a slideshow format that disappears after 24-hours. Yet, how did the candidates utilize the Instagram Story technology affordances, such as location tags, stickers, swipe up/websites, and hashtags? What political messages – attack, behind the scenes, or rally - did the candidates use both before and after Election Day? How do the candidates differ in the Story messages? Through the technology affordances lens, we conduct a quantitative content analysis of Instagram Stories posted by Trump and Biden one week before and after Election Day 2020. Our findings reveal how the possible actions or affordances linked to the "Story" feature allow candidates to communicate and engage with users. We conclude by offering a set of industry recommendations when using Instagram Stories in campaigns.

Introduction

Since 2016, Instagram has exploded in popularity (Perrin and Anderson 2019), particularly with the launch of "Stories" (Hutchinson 2019). "Stories," or short images or videos, is a posting method found on all primary social media platforms – it is now ubiquitous. While the "Stories" feature differs somewhat on various platforms – they all employ a host of technology affordances or features, such as stickers, location tags, and polls. This study focuses specifically on Instagram "Stories," asking what technological features of Instagram Stories are used by the candidates during the 2020 presidential campaign. We also ask who candidates are featuring and what political messages are used in their Stories. The best approach to understanding Instagram Stories is through the affordance's perspective. Technological affordances are actions or functions that a technology makes easier or more possible. That is, Instagram Stories offers a set of affordances that "digitally-enables" users to visually express their political identities and opinions at a narrow-targeted audience with faster speed and lower cost than email or a website (see Earl and Kimport 2011). Indeed, many scholars have applied affordances theory to social media's digital properties and uses on various platforms (for reviews, see Bucher and Helmond 2018; Hafezieh and Eshraghian 2017; also see boyd 2011; Ellison et al. 2010; Vitak and Ellison 2013) but few have examined Instagram Stories with an affordance approach.

What are Instagram Stories?

Instagram Stories are a mobile-first platform and are considered an opportunity for individuals and campaigns to be more authentic, less polished, and "in the moment" (Barnhart 2020; Rozario-Ospino 2019). Each Story can be either a static image or a video shown for up to 15 seconds when pressed. In addition, Stories can either be standalone or a continuous video message that is strung together. There are numerous technology affordances that a campaign marketer can employ. For example, marketers can include digital stickers that can be added to images or videos, location geotags, interactive polling, and Story "swipe up" links, connecting users to external websites. In addition, marketers can gather usage metrics, mainly time spent viewing and interacting with the content (i.e., through replies or direct messages on Stories). Unlike other digital content, Instagram Stories also allow accounts to be found by potential voters who do not follow the account. Therefore, a political marketer can use either location or hashtag to be "picked" up or located in a user search.

Presently, however, little is known regarding how presidential candidates employ Instagram Stories to alter how they engage and share campaign information with users. Therefore, we systematically content analyze 304 Instagram Stories posted by Donald Trump (N = 66) and Joe Biden (N = 238) one week before and after Election Day (November 3, 2020). In each Story, the authors code for the presence of candidates, celebrities, and voters, the use of location tags, stickers, emojis, swipe up/websites, hashtags, and the candidates' campaign messages. This research seeks to broaden previous technology affordances research by examining how the candidates use the distinctive Stories' features and functions during the 2020 campaign to reach users and communicate their message.

An affordance approach

We apply affordance theory, as it allows an examination of the unique affordances (i.e., features or qualities) of Instagram Stories that other technologies, such as blogs or email, and social media platforms, such as Twitter or Facebook, may not offer. First coined in Gibson's (1979) work, the original affordance theory focuses on how individuals perceive objects around them to execute specific actions. Later applying this theory to human-computer interaction, Gaver (1991) illustrates the "technology affordances" theory by applying it when identifying electronic media properties. These properties influence what electronic media have to offer to the user (Gaver 1991, 1996). That is, what tasks or functions can someone execute with the technology, such as email and Instagram (Hutchby 2001; Majchrzak et al. 2013)? For example, email and Instagram have unique features. Email can be used to communicate via text, attach image or audio files, and share and receive documents to a targeted audience. Whereas Instagram can be used to communicate via visual images and video with entertaining and colorful filters (i.e., color, tint, or augmented reality effects), graphics, and interactive features to a broad audience.

Instagram's social media affordances

Presently, Instagram's unique properties have been examined by scholars in the context of why individuals use Instagram rather than Twitter or Facebook. Users are aware that the technological features of Instagram are unique, centering on pictures, images, and videos that allow the user to tell a story. For instance, Hurley (2019) demonstrates that Instagram users choose Instagram due to its unique tools, conceptualized as material, such as "liking" content, conceptual, such as sharing images of hobbies and lifestyle choices, and imaginary, such as self-presentation via emojis, digital flower-crowns and fairy-tale decorations, to identify and represent themselves visually. Shane-Simpson et al. (2018) report that college students preferred Instagram, rather than Facebook and Twitter, due to Instagram's visual features and ability to connect with others (see also Rosenbaum 2019).

Instagram's story affordance

Focusing specifically on the differences between Instagram's "feed" and Stories, Li et al. (2021) find that elite athletes crafted Stories for lively interaction, promotion, and sharing behind-the-scenes stories. In contrast, Instagram's feed was used to express opinions and viewpoints. Comparing Facebook and Instagram's features, a survey of social media users reported that Instagram's Stories increased likeability toward an advertisement more than static content on Facebook's wall and Instagram's feed (Belanche, Cenjor, and Pérez-Rueda 2019). Even the mainstream media have also begun to employ Instagram Stories as a novel way to report stories and connect with their audience (see Schmidt 2018). Most media outlets employ Stories, employing features such as photos, text, content externally edited, video, emojis, icons, and more, to introduce information in a concise package to drive traffic (Vazquez-Herreor, Direito-Rebollal, and Lopez-Garcia 2019).

Instagram and political communication

Most political officeholders and candidates have fully embraced Instagram in their political marketing communication strategy (Straus 2018). They utilize this platform primarily to construct and narrate their public personas. Indeed, a growing number of articles explore the visual role of Instagram in political communication in several countries (see Lalancette and Raynauld 2019; Liebhart and Bernhardt 2017; Pineda, Bellido-Pérez, and Barragán-Romero 2022; Towner and Muñoz 2018; Turnbull-Dugarte 2019). Much of this work analyzes the content candidates, parties, and officeholders post on Instagram, generally concluding that the platform is used as a tool for self-promotion, advertising, and communication (see Dobkiewicz 2019; Muñoz and Towner 2017; O'Connell 2018). Yet, there is limited research specifically on Instagram's Stories featuring political campaigning. The closest political communication research conducted thus far is that of Nashmi and Painter (2018) analysis of presidential primary candidates on Snapchat "Snaps" – an Instagram Story equivalent. Their work identified ten frames or candidate messages: candidate character, issue, attack, supporters, campaign event, media, celebrity or political endorsement, behind the scenes, motivation/promotion, and others. The most popular frames were supporters, character, campaign events, and behind the scenes.

Social media affordances in political campaigning

Few studies apply the affordance lens to political campaigning in the U.S. on social media platforms. Kreiss, Lawrence, and McGregor's (2018) interviews with campaign practitioners during the 2016 election reveal that campaigns utilized various social media platforms because one platform offered a unique affordance, whereas another platform lacked that affordance. As a result, campaigns must craft content that conforms to each platform's unique features to reflect best their candidates' personae and character – all to reach voters and journalists. For example, in the 2016 election, political campaigners noted that Instagram's features included image control and high engagement but did not allow posting direct, outside hyperlinks (only in the bio). Other practitioners said that Twitter's features had chronological tweets for campaign content, whereas Facebook posts were filtered based on an algorithm. Similarly, utilizing the 2016 U.S. campaign as a case study, Bossetta (2018) concludes that Facebook was mainly used as a campaign tool due to its features – public pages, searchable content, hyperlinking, and few restrictions on content. But Instagram, owned by Facebook, was not unique, offering similar, if not the same features. (For affordance in campaigning in the German context, see Stier et al. 2018).

Instagram story affordances in political campaigning

In visual storytelling, it is important to note who is the focus of the Story. During a political campaign, storytellers could include the candidate, campaign workers, voters, groups of voters, and celebrities/notables, as these actors often play a central role in the narration. Examining Snapchat use in the 2016 U.S. primaries, Nashmi and Painter (2018) found that most candidates, particularly Sanders, Rubio, and Kasich, were present in their snaps at least two-thirds of the time, except for Hillary Clinton. More often than not, candidates were also with supporters. Notably, Clinton was depicted with political and celebrity endorsers and her family more than the other candidates. Snaps, including campaign workers, made up a minimal number of Stories. Nashmi and Painter's (2018) findings are similar to numerous studies that examine the visual content political candidates post on Instagram. For example, Towner and Muñoz (2018) note that the 2016 presidential primary candidates posted Instagram images with children, family, celebrities, admiring individuals, and large audiences, all to exude "statesmanship" and "compassion" to users (see also Liebhart and Bernhardt 2017; Turnbull-Dugarte 2019). In the context of Instagram Stories in the 2020 campaign, we ask: *RQ1. Who was the focus of the candidates' Instagram Story?*

As Bossetta (2018), Kreiss, Lawrence, and McGregor (2018), and other scholars discuss, Instagram offers various technology features. Stories' features include animated stickers, location stickers, emoji's, swipe up/website, and the use of image or video. As we noted, there is little research examining Instagram Stories in political campaigning. Therefore, we draw on Nashmi and Painter (2018) work focusing on the 2016 U.S. presidential primary candidates' SnapChat posts. Examining Snapchat, the authors explored the production techniques or features, particularly whether the format of each snap (static photo or video), camera movement (still or moving), and the presence or absence of captions and filters. Their findings revealed that most candidates – Clinton, Rubio, and Kasich, but not Sanders – used videos in a majority of snaps and included camera movement. These candidates did not often use geo-location or election filters (i.e., digital "I Voted" sticker), but 70% inserted captions in their snaps. Given these findings, candidates are indeed using the technological features on these social media platforms. We, therefore, ask: *RQ2. What affordances do the 2020 presidential candidates' Instagram Stories employ?*

Instagram's affordances enable candidates to tell a visual story with tellers and, most importantly, a message. Political research has long examined the messages delivered by candidates and campaigns via digital platforms (see Bichard 2006; Parmelee and Bichard 2012; Towner 2016; Trammell et al. 2006; Wicks and Souley 2003). Similar analyses have been conducted on Instagram posts. For example, Pineda, Bellido-Pérez, and Barragán-Romero (2022) find that Spanish political leaders post about the party's stance, leader positioning, non-electoral promotion of the leader/party, personal information, acknowledgments, and more. Liebhart and Bernhardt (2017) study of Alexander Van der Bellen's Instagram account reveals posts mainly about the campaign, media work, fan contact, call to action, and background stories. Adapting Nashmi and Painter (2018) work, finding that the 2016 U.S. presidential candidates used various types of political messages in their snaps, we ask: *RQ3: What was the main political message captured in the candidates' Story?*

To better understand Stories' current communication norms, political marketers should turn to the "best practices" of traditional brands. A review of industry articles on Instagram Stories from Social Media Examiner (i.e., a leading industry educational outlet devoted to social media) and popular social media monitoring software companies, Agorapulse, Hootsuite, and Sprout Social identified a series of suggestions related to content type and technology features. Content suggestions sought to capitalize on the brand's opportunity to be authentic by offering "behind the scenes" footage. Other industry advice recommends sharing user-generated content (UGC), offering how-to, tutorials, deals and promotions, and special announcements (Barnhart 2020). Within this list, "behind the scenes stories" and sharing user-generated content are the most appropriate for political campaigns—many of the industry suggestions revolved around technology features. The specific features recommended, description and benefits of the tool can be found in Table 1 (Barnhart 2020; Beadon 2020; Cooper 2020; Gotter 2020). *RQ4: To what extent do the 2020 presidential candidates conform to Instagram Story industry best practices?*

Table 1. Media affordances on Instagram.

Media affordances	Description	Benefit
Interactive stickers	These types of Stickers ask for a response. They include polls, chat, questions, and countdowns	Consumer engagement Sense of community Market research
Stickers – General	There are many types of general stickers, ranging from an assortment of emojis to colorful text. There are also donation and product purchase stickers	Creative Reinforces Message Allows for purchases Allows for donations
Location – Stickers	Physical location is placed on the sticker	Find story in explore Sense of community
Hashtag – Sticker and text	Graphic Sticker or written text that includes a hashtag (#) before the text	Find story in explore Connects to issue
Text/Text overlays	This includes both written text on a static image or video and transcript of audio posted on video	Increase the likelihood that the message is understood Accessibility
Handle/Tag	Denotes another account by tagging with a @. Often used when reposting material. You can also tag with Stickers	Build community Creates exposure for another account/reshare
Swipe Up	A Swipe-Up option is provided, taking consumers to the specific website. Accounts need 10,000 followers for "Swipe-Up" option to be available	Direct call to action Consumer engagement
Video	Video lasting up to 15 seconds. Longer video can be segmented into shorter segments.	Increase potential exposure in explore Consumer engagement

Methodology

To address the research questions, two weeks of Instagram Stories (October 27-November 10, 2020) were downloaded from the joebiden and teamtrump Instagram accounts and analyzed. The week before the Tuesday, November 3, 2020, presidential election was examined, as we expected more Stories to be posted immediately before Election Day. We also analyze the week following Election Day, as the election was not "called" until November 7, 2020. While Joe Biden only had one Instagram account at the time of analysis, we acknowledge that President Trump had two verified Instagram accounts: realdonaldtrump and teamtrump. The realdonaldtrump account is positioned as his "official" Presidential account with the description: "45th President of the United States". The teamtrump account is focused on his reelection bid and managed by his campaign. Given that our focus was on campaign communications, we examine the Instagram account dedicated to the campaign: teamtrump.

In total, 304 Stories were downloaded using the 4 K Stogram program (Biden N = 238; Trump N = 66).[1] Each Story was treated as a separate unit of analysis. In some instances, chronological images and video were separated into different Stories; however, they were analyzed independently. If the Story format was a video, the entire length of the video was watched. Video, audio, and text overlay on the video were included in the analysis to clarify further. Stories were evaluated based on the type of technology features used, individuals included, and dominant message type. Message types were drawn and adapted primarily from Nashmi and Painter (2018) 2016 U.S. presidential primary Snapchat research. Nine of the ten original message types were used: candidate character (i.e., voter interaction with candidate and candidate participating in regular activities), issue, attack, campaign event, hybrid media (i.e., media appearances and depicting other forms of media, such as Twitter), endorsements (i.e., politician, celebrity, and focused supporters), behind the scenes (i.e., planning and prepping campaign-related activities), motivation (or mobilization) (i.e., providing a call to action), and other. In contrast, to Nashmi and Painter's (2018) work, the category of "supporters" was included in campaign events/rallies when they were included in event crowds. Supporters were also classified as voter endorsements when they were singled out in Stories carrying or wearing campaign posters/merchandise. An additional category of "Thank You," in which candidates offer their gratitude toward voters, was added based on Muñoz and Towner's (2017) Instagram research. The coding of the message categories remained the same in our study, with some exceptions.[2] In the Fall of 2020, the Covid-19

Pandemic was active. We added two subcategories, particularly "Pandemic" and "Presence of Masks," of the "Issue" message type to determine how information related to the pandemic was communicated. If the message types did not represent a Story, it was coded as "Other." After the initial analysis, further analysis was done to identify new message types represented in the "Other" category.

Stories were coded with items being present or not present. In some instances, multiple message types were assigned. This often occurred when political messages were set at campaign events/rallies. Two trained coders evaluated the entire dataset. To determine inter-rater reliability, Cohen's Kappa was used (see Table 2). Most all of the items had a "substantial" or "near-perfect" agreement. Author disagreements were discussed and revised.

Results

An analysis of the joebiden and teamtrump's Instagram Stories revealed that the Biden campaign (N = 238) was considerably more active than Trump's campaign (N = 66) in posting Stories. Both campaigns significantly reduced the number of Stories posted after Election Day – despite the election not being "called" until Saturday, November 7, 2020. From November 5 until the 10, Biden's campaign posted only eight stories, whereas Trump's campaign posted ten. Table 2 provides the descriptive results.

RQ1. Who was the focus of the candidates' Instagram Story?

The candidate was the primary focus of both accounts Stories (Biden = 63.9%; Trump = 71.2%). Candidates were both depicted walking to and from vehicles/airplanes, approaching

Table 2. Results.

	Biden (n = 238)	Biden %	Trump (n = 66)	Trump %	Cohen's Kappa
Media affordances					
Video	155	65.1	47	71.2	.978
Text	231	97.1	41	62.1	.983
Hashtag	0	0	1	1.5	.665
Handle	5	2.1	1	1.5	.662
Location Sticker	3	1.3	2	3	.966
Sticker – General	2	.84	8	12.1	.563
Poll/Interactive	0	0	0	0	n/a
"Swipe Up"	6	2.5	15	21.2	.971
Other account/Feature	13	5.5	4	6.1	.904
Individuals/Group					
Candidate	152	63.9	47	71.2	1
Voter group	31	13	8	13.6	.941
Voters	22	9.2	10	15.6	.966
Campaign workers	2	.8	5	7.6	.897
Children	4	1.7	5	7.6	.744
Celebrity	26	10.9	3	4.5	.942
Message types					
Campaign event/rally	125	52.5	39	59.1	1
Thank you	15	6.3	2	3	.968
Voter endorsement	7	2.9	8	12.1	.966
Issues	39	16.4	12	18.2	.964
Pandemic	8	3.4	0	0	1
Mask	82	34.9	11	16.7	.925
Hybrid/Media	0	0	12	18.2	1
Character	7	2.9	0	0	.76
Attack	31	13	5	7.6	.984
Behind the scenes	3	1.26	0	0	.498
Mobilization	57	24	18	27.3	.937
Other	59	24.8	1	1.5	.958
Unity	16	6.7	0	0	1
Motivational	10	4.2	0	0	1

podiums, and on stage. Yet, the most common type of appearance was that of the candidate at a rally and giving a speech. Trump's Stories included both him at the podium or stage speaking, with crowds in the background or panned crowd shots. In contrast, Biden's Stories were primarily focused on him at the podium/stage. None of Trump's Stories had him directly talking to the camera, whereas Biden only spoke directly to the camera once. Outside of the candidates themselves, voters or voter groups were shown holding signs, and some offered video endorsements. Children were seen as members of the audience and with, presumably, their parents. Kayleigh McEnany's (Trump's press secretary) child was in four of the five Trump Stories depicting children. Celebrities or notable politicians endorsed candidates (e.g., Lady Gaga and President Obama for Biden). They also were depicted in negative perspectives (e.g., Biden policy comparison with Donald Trump; Trump showing an image of Andrew Cuomo and the headline "Gov. Andrew Cuomo threatens to block Trump admin's distribution of Covid Vaccine").

RQ2: What technology affordances do the 2020 presidential candidates' Instagram Stories employ?

Overall, each campaign did not frequently apply the variety of Instagram Stories' technology features. Both Biden and Trump used video in a majority of their Stories. However, the Trump campaign was considerably less likely to include text (62%), in either static images or video, than Biden (97%). In addition, neither campaign readily utilized location stickers or hashtags. Trump's campaign was, however, more likely to use general stickers compared to Biden. These stickers encouraged users to vote for Trump (e.g., a pulsing "I'm voting for Trump" sticker in the corner and block letter "MAGA" repeatedly spelling out at the top).

Account handles of other accounts were also rarely included, and none of them used the Instagram text feature, allowing the tagged individual to share on their accounts. Content from other Instagram accounts was seldom used. When content was repurposed for Stories, it most often came from either Biden or Trump's main Instagram feed or "Reels." "Reels" are short, 3 to 15-second video clips with audio, effects, and other special features. Both campaigns also did not take the opportunity to engage with viewers directly. Interactive polling or question stickers were not included for either campaign. Lastly, only the Trump campaign readily used the "Swipe Up" feature that allows viewers to go directly to a designated website. These were most commonly used in conjunction with hybrid media Stories. Biden's campaign would often list a website on a Story but not provide the direct means to visit through the technology features.

RQ3. What was the main political message captured in the candidates' Story?

Despite the significant differences in the candidate's platforms, their communication messaging and Story location (i.e., campaign event/rally) were similar in several ways. The most popular type of message type for both Biden and Trump was mobilization. Candidates sought to have voters create a voting plan (Biden), attend virtual events – artist collaboration for telephone political posters (Biden), get out the vote messaging (Biden and Trump), visit iwillvote.com (Biden), text voter sign-ups (Trump), and help stop election fraud (Trump). Both candidates also included several policy issues in their Stories. Specifically, Biden focused primarily on healthcare, the pandemic, and the economy. Black Lives Matter/Black rights, education, climate, gun regulations, democracy, and science were also included. Whereas Trump primarily focused on the economy. Other issues, such as immigration, military, anti-socialism, pandemic, and voter fraud, were also present. Trump highlighting the economy's strength, whereas Biden focusing his efforts primarily on the pandemic and healthcare is one marked difference between campaigns. The priorities of the campaign related to the pandemic were also implicitly communicated through mask-wearing. Approximately 35% of Biden's Stories depicted most, if not all, of the individuals wearing masks. Whereas only 17% of Trump's Stories included most individuals wearing masks, and often the United States Secret Service only wore them.

Additional points of similarity between the campaigns can be found in the lack of specific content area messaging. Notably, Trump did not offer any behind-the-scenes Stories. In contrast, the Biden campaign only showed three: Stories with Biden getting out of a vehicle and another where he is speaking directly to the camera in what appears to be an event's setup. Stories that spoke to the candidate's character by elaborating on their family, hobbies, and interests were also primarily absent by both campaigns. Trump's Stories offered none, whereas the Biden campaign Stories mentioned Biden's family, specifically his son Beau, in a relatively small number. Lastly, both campaigns took few opportunities to thank their supporters. When this occurred, it was done either at a rally podium or in-text overlay to images and video. Most often, they were thanking cities that they had visited.

Outside of differences in issues prioritized, the campaigns differed the most on voter endorsement, hybrid media, attack, and "other" messaging types. Trump's campaign took more opportunities to capture voter endorsements. These voter endorsements were almost all video, emotion-laden Stories. Often one voter endorsement spanned multiple Stories, conveying a personal story as to why individuals were voting for Trump. Each of Trump's video endorsements was made by minority voters. In contrast, Biden presented only static images of voters and voter groups holding signs of support. This included one Story of Lady Gaga holding on to a Biden campaign button. No celebrity endorsements were found in Trump Stories. Another difference is found in Trump presenting media reports from newspapers, television shows, and tweets in Instagram Stories. Uniquely, the hybrid media Story would include a static image, the media headline or primary takeaway in large font, the logo of the news source, and a swipe-up button to presumably access the source. Examples of hybrid media topics include "U.S. GDP Booms at 33.1% rate in Q3, better than expected (CNBC)," and "Report: Half of Trump's Twitter and Facebook posts since election day flagged as misinformation (Breitbart)."

In the attack messaging, Biden presented more negative or comparison Story content about Trump. Some of the Story content was negative statements expressed in speeches. In other instances, Biden created charts outlining the differences between his policies and Trump's on a host of issues. Trump varied in his approach. His account expressed negative views on Biden within a speech, tweet, press release, and a sharing of a magazine article. Finally, perhaps the most notable difference between the candidates is simply the diversity of messages that the Biden campaign provided in Stories compared to Team Trump. In total, 25% of Biden's Stories had unique message content that did not conform to our established content types. An additional independent review by both coders found eleven additional message types. The most popular type of Story revolved around the messaging of unity. Repeatedly, through both Biden's spoken remarks and written text overlays, the emphasis was on a nation united. "Motivational" Stories was another often-repeated theme. These types of Stories include quotes like "Keep the Faith" Stories from the post-election speech regarding their thoughts on whether they won, and a video of pastoral views of a diverse United States with accompanying music "America the Beautiful." Other types of Story messaging that occurred less frequently included: Campaign Trial, Personal Appeals, Middle-Class Appeals, Entertainment (games to do while in the voting line), Our Future, Humor, Election fraud, Branding, and Patriotism.

RQ4. To what extent do the 2020 presidential candidates conform to Story industry best practices?

Industry best practices focus on viewing Stories as a means to provide authentic and creative messaging. Neither Biden nor the Trump campaign appeared to embrace the Story communication norms. There was little attempt to speak directly to the camera. Each campaign only offered one occasion when an individual spoke directly to the camera (Biden and Kayleigh McEnany for Trump). In addition, many of the Stories were readily just taken at rally events filming the candidates speaking with minimal, if any, editing or technology features added. Stories were prominently "front-stage" candidate perspectives – they did not offer "behind the scenes" or personal glimpses of their life outside of being a political candidate. That said, there were a small number of creative Stories. For example, a montage of Trump dancing on-stage to YMCA with moving MAGA stickers and Biden including a "Reels" adapted paper storyboard. Yet, some of these were designed originally for other mediums ("Reels"), and others could have been repurposed Instagram and Facebook feed posts. For example, Biden's campaign posted a series of "entertainment" Stories for people to view while in the voter line. These consisted of word searches and "find-and-seek" object posts that could not be accomplished in the fifteen seconds. Other posts, such as Biden's "attack" policy comparisons, could not entirely be read in a Story's length. Other markers of creativity, such as photo or face filters, stickers, and informal written text on images, were absent. User-generated content, another marketer recommended content type, from voters was also not apparent.

The uniqueness of Instagram Stories, outside of its short length and ephemeral nature, is primarily attributed to their technology features. Yet, both campaigns rarely used them. On a more basic technology features level, both Biden and Trump embraced video. However, Trump did not always utilize text in his posts. Given that many users have sound turned off while watching Stories (Patel 2016), this is a missed opportunity. In contrast, Biden readily included text, including transcripts of speeches. Both candidates also missed opportunities to be included in the Instagram search feature explore by not often including location stickers or hashtags. They also did not fully engage potential voters through engagement polls or questions. One of marketers' most valuable technology features, "Swipe Up," was also not used frequently – although Trump made much more use of it than Biden.

Discussion

Despite the millions spent on social media marketing, both the Biden and Trump campaigns faltered when utilizing Instagram Stories. They did not subscribe to the communication norms of the platform nor follow best practices set by marketers. Therefore, how should political marketers use Stories in their political campaigns? Drawing upon industry recommendations (Barnhart 2020; Beadon 2020; Cooper 2020; Gotter 2020) and the authors' analysis of multiple Story datasets, the following discussion contextualizes our findings in the literature and then concludes with suggestions to effectively employ Instagram Stories in political communication strategy (see Table 3 for an overview).

Consistent with previous social media campaigns (i.e., Lalancette and Raynauld 2019; Liebhart and Bernhardt 2017; Turnbull-Dugarte 2019), it is not surprising that the candidate is the main storyteller (R.Q. #1). Both Biden and Trump used Instagram Stories to communicate their political personalities and manage their political image. Notably, there was little blurring of the boundaries between their personal/private and political/professional lives. Biden and Trump focused their Stories entirely on their political selves, primarily with stump speeches, rallies, and events. Indeed, these Stories are posted at the general election's finish line. Still, neither candidate offered Stories that transcended the professional and bureaucratic nature of political communications commonplace in mainstream political communications. There were no personal pleas to followers to "vote for me" before (or on) Election Day, and there were few direct "thank you" for your support following Election Day. Both Biden and Trump included some personal elements in their Stories, including photos and videos of family members on the campaign trail. These Stories also illustrate that these candidates carefully (and infrequently) used celebrities and notables in their campaign narrative. Celebrities were rarely pictured or recorded without the candidate. There were no celebrity "Instagram Takeovers." These findings suggest that the campaigns felt no benefit from a celebrity endorser late in the campaign. Perhaps celebrities were not viewed as an authentic or genuine part of their Story's narrative. Overall, Biden and Trump centered their Stories on themselves.

The content analysis of features reveals that the candidates were not actively using Instagram Stories to their full potential (R.Q. #2). Instagram Stories afforded candidates the ability to upload photos and video, and then add fun and engaging content such as stickers (e.g., GIFs, time of day, questions, music, poll, countdowns), location stickers, swipe up/websites, hashtags (e.g., #election2020), and handles (e.g., @ladygaga). Biden and Trump largely eschewed these Story features and relied on text. Indeed, both candidates included a fair amount of video in

Table 3. Political story content type ideas.

Content type	Description	Political application	Media affordance
How-To/Tutorial	Stories that provide instructions to viewers	Instructions for how to register to vote; register for absentee vote; check to confirm whether vote was processed; set up virtual watch party; train volunteers, set up a carpool to vote	"Swipe Up" to the dedicated website
Promotion	Stories that promote merchandise and events	Promote and sell campaign hats, buttons, signs, stickers, posters, and clothing. Promote debates, political talks, media appearances, and fundraisers.	Provide buy sticker and "Swipe Up" option Location Sticker for event
Education	Stories that educate about the candidate's policy platform	Provide statistics related to specific policies. Provide quotes supporting candidate's policy. Provide candidate quote on policy. Question and Answer sessions. Information on how government/process works	Hashtag related to policy; "Swipe Up" to the dedicated website.
Mobilization	Stories that seek to get viewers to act	Reminders related to voting; Information on where to go vote; Sign-Ups for Volunteering; Donation requests; Call other politicians and public offices	Voting and donation related stickers "Swipe Up" to the dedicated website
Media	Stories that profile other media	Images recapping positive candidate press coverage from television, newspaper, and magazines. Tweets from candidate, notable individuals, and voters; negative media information regarding competitor	Hashtag sticker "Swipe Up" to media website
Campaign events	Stories that capture campaign events	Images and video of event crowds, speeches, and music.	Location sticker
Influencers/ Celebrity	Stories that include influencers/celebrities	Images or video of influencer, celebrity, or another political candidate discussing and/or endorsing candidate and encouraging GOTV; influencer takeover of account	Hashtag sticker Handle
Behind the scenes	Stories that provide insight into planning and nonprofessional life.	Images or video of the candidate at home, exercising, pets, current and historical family images, in car, off-stage, outside, dressed casually, eating/drinking, and participating in a hobby. Informal office images	Location sticker Hashtag sticker
User-generated content	Stories that other users create	Images or video of voter endorsements, voter experiences at events	Hashtag sticker Handle

the Stories, but this was primarily unedited/unfiltered videos of stump speeches and rallies. The candidates mostly used swipe ups (for websites), handles, and a few stickers. In sum, by not building on Instagram's affordances, Biden and Trump's Instagram Stories looked very similar to their Instagram posts.

Regarding R.Q. #3, similar to Nashmi and Painter's (2018) research, supporters were present in Stories' ample campaign events. Campaign events and rallies were the most popular types of messages. Voter support was most notably seen in Trump's campaign events where large crowd shots were readily shown. One potential reason for the size and depiction of campaign crowds varying between campaigns may be attributed mainly to the Biden campaign employing social distancing strategies (e.g., car crowds and mask-wearing). Masks were primarily absent in Trump's Stories, and supporters were depicted close to each other in crowds. In general, the Trump campaign did a good job conveying voter support through crowd and individualized video endorsements. Biden's campaign should have concentrated much more of its efforts on voter support outside of static images.

While Nashmi and Painter (2018) found that a candidate's character was one of the most popular frames, we found little to no Stories that revealed personal information and voter interaction revealing character. Much of this may be attributed to the Covid pandemic that minimized voter interactions; however, it does not account for the lack of personal details revealed. "Behind the Scenes" Stories were also seen in less frequency compared to the Snapchat study. Other significant contrasts in the two studies can be found in the Instagram Stories emphasis on Mobilization and Issues. Approximately a quarter of Stories focused on mobilizing voters, ranging from GOTV efforts to texting. This increased emphasis may be attributed to advances in technology features in the Stories platform. Nevertheless, both campaigns did not effectively integrate technology features, such as the "swipe up" feature, that increase the likelihood of their requested action being completed.

Campaign issues were mentioned through stump speeches, newspaper articles, and infographics. The increased reliance that voters have on social media for news, coupled with the larger and slightly older Instagram user base, may explain the difference between Snaps and Stories. Attack messaging varied between the 2016 Snapchat candidates and Biden and Trump's Stories. Biden's more frequent attack messaging may be attributed to the slightly more sophisticated lineup of Stories. In addition to providing more Stories, Biden created comparison charts contrasting his policy stances to Trump's. Regarding media messaging, Trump's campaign Stories were consistent with previous political Snaps; however, Biden's campaigns offered no Stories depicting other media articles/sources. Lastly, the diversity of Biden's political messaging was also unique. Some of the political messaging was tied into the overarching campaign message (i.e., unity in our nation). In contrast, other messaging was attributed to current events (i.e., election fraud and "keep the faith" motivational posts) that had the Trump campaign questioning the election process.

Both campaigns did not consistently follow Instagram Story communication norms and marketing industry advice (R.Q. #4). To begin, the frequency and consistency of posting Stories should have been more substantial. In particular, Team Trump provided a relatively small number of Stories; however, both campaigns needed to be more consistent, especially after the election. Given the ambiguity after the U.S. Presidential Election Day, more communication should have been delivered. Outside of the frequency of post creation, campaigns did not considerably vary in their content type. Both concentrated their efforts on campaign events and provided very few personal or behind-the-scenes viewpoints into their campaign. Glimpses of home life, pets, backstage footage, exercising, old family photos, and hobbies serve to humanize the candidate and conform to the communication norms that viewers expect within the Story format. This lack of "backstage" or exclusive content runs counter to both consumer and industry Story expectations. Other content types such as mobilization, issues, and media were applied by one or both campaigns with varying degrees of success. Some of these Stories lacked proper features (i.e., swipe up), whereas others did not seem to be constructed originally for the Stories platform. While Biden's campaign provided the most diversity in content types, some Stories were not originally designed to be Stories. Another missed opportunity by both campaigns was the lack of user-generated content – there was little evidence that they regramed content from the voters. They could have repurposed voter footage, received additional endorsements from celebrities, and even had a campaign worker or celebrity "takeover" their account for the day. In general, both campaigns did not generate consistently strong or diverse Story content. For examples of other political Story content-type ideas, see Table 3.

Beyond content, Biden and Trump's Stories did not effectively utilize technology affordances, except for their frequent video and text use. Most notably, Stories lacked interactive stickers, location and hashtag stickers, and text. Both campaigns should have had a location sticker for each event and hashtags related to policies; these efforts would increase the likelihood of new potential voters finding Stories in explore. Tagging other users also expands a candidate's reach. Interactive stickers, such as polling, question answering, and chat, could have provided market research and community engagement. Donation stickers could have directly raised money for the campaigns – yet they were not used. Lastly, creative uses of technology features through scribed text and stickers were also not present. Overall, the sense of creativity and "fun" that often define Stories were mostly absent from these accounts.

Limitations

The ephemeral nature of Instagram Stories makes this content challenging to examine. We overcame this barrier by downloading and saving each Story for the two presidential candidates. This manual data collection was limited in some ways. For instance, when Stories indicated a "swipe up" feature, we could not view the content linked to the Story after the Story was downloaded and stored. A larger sample including Stories posted by other candidates, media outlets, political parties, voters, and so forth would offer a different perspective on Stories told during the 2020 campaign. Other limitations include the electoral context in 2020 and the limited period (i.e., two weeks) of Story collection. We acknowledge that we cannot generalize Biden and Trump's Stories to other candidates' Stories.

Future research

To gain a broader understanding of Instagram Stories, a future project should examine officeholders' and politicians' Instagram Stories in a non-election period. A future project should assess if these same Instagram Stories are posted on additional social media platforms. That is, are candidates crafting different Stories on various platforms to reach different target audiences? Are the features the same or similar on these platforms? Is the Story's message the same across platforms? In conclusion, consumers view Stories because they want authenticity, which goes beyond the often posed, photo edited traditional Instagram posts. This is an opportunity for campaigns to give potential voters insider perspectives and creative messaging. Unfortunately, both the Biden and Trump campaigns largely missed this opportunity. Candidates should focus not just on mobilizing efforts added by technology affordances (i.e., swipe up), but also prioritize "behind the scenes" Stories. Also, candidates must utilize technology features. Lastly, Stories need to be creatively personalized for each candidate. Stickers, GIFs, and filters are some of the many ways to make Instagram content fun and engaging. In the end, it is up to the campaign to tell a good story, even if it is a short one.

Notes

1. To avoid sampling error, we did not draw a random sample of Stories. Instead, we content analyzed all Stories posted by the candidates. We acknowledge that more Biden Instagram Stories (N= 238) are being examined than Trump's Instagram Stories (N = 66).
2. Our study referred to the "Motivational" category as "Mobilization." The "Media" category was expanded to include not just media appearances but also "Hybrid" forms of media – depicting images of other forms of media (i.e., Tweets, newspaper articles, etc.).

References

Barnhart, B. 2020. "Instagram Stories: Best Practices for Your Brand." https://sproutsocial.com/insights/instagram-stories/

Beadon, A. 2020. "How to Convert Leads Using Instagram Stories." https://www.socialmediaexaminer.com/how-to-convert-leads-using-instagram-stories/

Belanche, D., I. Cenjor, and A. Pérez-Rueda. 2019. "Instagram Stories versus Facebook Wall: An Advertising Effectiveness Analysis." *Spanish Journal of Marketing – ESIC* 23 (1):69–94. doi: 10.1108/SJME-09-2018-0042.

Bichard, S. L. 2006. "Building Blogs: A Multi-Dimensional Analysis of the Distribution of Frames on the 2004 Presidential Candidate Web Sites." *Journalism & Mass Communication Quarterly* 83 (2):329–45. doi: 10.1177/107769900608300207.

Bossetta, M. 2018. "The Digital Architectures of Social Media: Comparing Political Campaigning on Facebook, Twitter, Instagram, and Snapchat in the 2016 U.S. Election." *Journalism & Mass Communication Quarterly* 95 (2):471–96. doi: 10.1177/1077699018763307.

boyd, d. 2011. "Social Network Sites as Networked Publics: Affordances, Dynamics, and Implications." In *A Networked Self: Identity, Community, and Culture on Social Network Sites*, edited by Z. Papacharissi, 39–58. New York, NY: Routledge Taylor and Francis Group. doi: 10.4324/9780203876527.

Bucher, T., and A. Helmond. 2018. "The Affordances of Social Media Platforms." In *The SAGE Handbook of Social Media*, edited by J. Burgess, A. Marwick, and T. Poell, 233–53. London, England: SAGE.

Cooper, P. 2020. "How to Use Instagram Stories to Build Your Audience." https://blog.hootsuite.com/how-to-use-instagram-stories/

Dobkiewicz, P. 2019. "Instagram Narratives in Trump's." *Journal of Language and Politics* 18 (6):826–47. doi: 10.1075/jlp.19039.dob.

Earl, J., and K. Kimport. 2011. *Digitally Enabled Social Change: Activism in the Internet Age.* Cambridge, MA; London, England: The MIT Press. doi: 10.2307/j.ctt5hhcb9.

Ellison, N., C. Lampe, C. Steinfield, and J. Vitak. 2010. "With a Little Help from my Friends: Social Network Sites and Social Capital." In *A Networked Self: Identity, Community and Culture on Social Network Sites*, Z. Papacharissi, 124–45. New York: Routledge.

Gaver, W. W. 1996. "Situating Action II: Affordances for Interaction: The Social is Material for Design." *Ecological Psychology* 8 (2):111–29. doi: 10.1207/s15326969eco0802_2.

Gaver, W. W. 1991. "Technology Affordances." Proceedings of the SIGCHI Conference on Human Factors in Computing Systems Reaching through Technology – CHI '91: 79–84." https://dl.acm.org/doi/10.1145/108844.108856.

Gibson, J. J. 1979. "The Theory of Affordances." In *The Ecological Approach to Visual Perception*, J. J. Gibson, 119–36. Boston, MA: Houghton Mifflin.

Gotter, A. 2020. "7 Best Practices to Rock Your Instagram Stories." https://www.agorapulse.com/blog/best-practices-instagram-stories/

Hafezieh, N., and F. Eshraghian. 2017. "Affordance Theory in Social Media Research: Systematic Review and Synthesis of the Literature." Presented at the 25th European Conference on Information Systems, ECIS 2017. https://ssrn.com/abstract=2988394.

Hutchinson, A. 2019. "Instagram Stories is Now Being Used by 500 Million People Daily." *Social Media Today.* https://www.socialmediatoday.com/news/instagram-stories-is-now-beingused-by-500-million-people-daily/547270/

Hutchby, I. 2001. "Technologies, Texts and Affordances." *Sociology* 35 (2):441–56. doi: 10.1177/S0038038501000219.

Hurley, Z. 2019. "Imagined Affordances of Instagram and the Fantastical Authenticity of Female Gulf-Arab Social Media Influencers." *Social Media + Society* 59(1). https://doi.org/10.1177/2056305118819241.

Kreiss, D., R. G. Lawrence, and S. C. McGregor. 2018. "In Their Own Words: Political Practitioner Accounts of Candidates, Audiences, Affordances, Genres, and Timing in Strategic Social Media Use." *Political Communication* 35 (1):8–31. doi: 10.1080/10584609.2017.1334727.

Lalancette, M., and V. Raynauld. 2019. "The Power of Political Image: Justin Trudeau, Instagram, and Celebrity Politics." *American Behavioral Scientist* 63 (7):888–924. doi: 10.1177/0002764217744838.

Li, B., O. K.M. Scott, M. Naraine, and B. J. Ruihley. 2021. "Tell Me a Story: Exploring Elite Female Athletes' Self-Presentation via an Analysis of Instagram Stories." *Journal of Interactive Advertising* 21 (2):108–20. doi: 10.1080/15252019.2020.1837038.

Liebhart, K., and P. Bernhardt. 2017. "Political Storytelling on Instagram: Key Aspects of Alexander Van Der Bellen's Successful 2016 Presidential Election Campaign." *Media and Communication* 5 (4):15–25. doi: 10.17645/mac.v5i4.1062.

Majchrzak, A., S. Faraj, G.C. Kane, and B. Azad. 2013. "The Contradictory Influence of Social Media Affordances on Online Communal Knowledge Sharing." *Journal of Computer-Mediated Communication* 19:38–55. doi: 10.1111/jcc4.12030.

Muñoz, C. L., and T. L. Towner. 2017. "The Image is the Message: Instagram Marketing and the 2016 Presidential Primary Season." *Journal of Political Marketing* 16 (3–4):290–318. doi: 10.1080/15377857.2017.1334254.

Nashmi, E. A., and D. Painter. 2018. "Oh Snap : ChatStyle in the 2016 U.S. Presidential Primaries." *Journal of Creative Communications* 13 (1):17–33. doi: 10.1177/0973258617743619.

O'Connell, D. 2018. "#Selfie: Instagram and the United States Congress." *Social Media + Society* 4 (4) 205630511881337. doi: 10.1177/2056305118813373.

Parmelee, J. H., and S. L. Bichard. 2012. *Politics and the Twitter Revolution: How Tweets Influence the Relationship between Political Leaders and the Public.* Lanham, MD: Lexington Books.

Patel, S. 2016. "85 Percent of Facebook Video is Watched without Sound." *Digiday.* https://digiday.com/media/silent-world-facebook-video/

Perrin, A, and M. Anderson. 2019. "Share of U.S. Adults using social media, including Facebook, is mostly since 2018." *Pew Research Center.* https://www.pewresearch.org/fact-tank/2019/04/10/share-of-u-s-adults-using-social-media-including-facebook-is-mostly-unchanged-since-2018/

E. Bellido-Pérez, and A. I. Barragán-Romero. 2022. "Backstage moments during the campaign": The interactive use of Instagram by Spanish political leaders." *New Media and Society* 24 (5):1133–1160. doi: 10.1177/1461444820972390.

Rosenbaum, J. E. 2019. "Degrees of Freedom: Exploring Agency, Narratives, and Technological Affordances in the #TakeAKnee Controversy." *Social Media + Society* doi: 10.1177/2056305119826125.

Rozario-Ospino, J. 2019. "Instagram Stories vs. Instagram Feed: What to Post and Where [Infographic]." *Social Media Today.* https://www.socialmediatoday.com/news/instagram-stories-vs-instagram-feed-what-to-post-and-where-infographic/556205/.

Stier, S., A. Bleier, H. Lietz, and M. Strohmaier. 2018. "Election Campaigning on Social Media: Politicians, Audiences, and the Mediation of Political Communication on Facebook and Twitter." *Political Communication* 35 (1):50–74. doi: 10.1080/10584609.2017.1334728.

Schmidt, C. 2018. "The Cincinnati Enquirer wrote an audience-driven article using Instagram Stories (and it wasn't even about a hippo)." *Nieman Lab.* http://www.niemanlab.org/2018/08/the-cincinnati-enquirer-wrote-an-audience-driven-article-using-instagram-stories-and-it-wasnt-even-about-a-hippo/

Shane-Simpson, C., A. Manago, N. Gaggi, and K. Gillespie-Lynch. 2018. "Why Do College Students Prefer Facebook, Twitter, or Instagram? Site Affordances, Tensions between Privacy and Self-Expression, and Implications for Social Capital." *Computers in Human Behavior* 86:276–88. doi: 10.1016/j.chb.2018.04.041.

Straus, J. 2018. "Social Media Adoption by Members of Congress: Trends and Congressional Considerations." *Congressional Research Service*: 1–21. https://fas.org/sgp/crs/misc/R45337.pdf.

Towner, T. L. 2016. "The Influence of Twitter Posts on Candidate Perceptions: The 2014 Michigan Midterms." In *Communication and Mid-Term Elections: Media, Message, and Mobilization*, edited by J. A. Hendricks and D. Schill, 145–67. New York: Palgrave.

Towner, T. L., and C. L. Muñoz. 2018. "Picture Perfect? The Role of Instagram in Issue Agenda Setting during the 2016 Presidential Primary Campaign." *Social Science Computer Review* 36 (4):484–99. doi: 10.1177/0894439317728222.

Trammell, K. D., A. P. Williams, M. Postelnicu, and K. D. Landreville. 2006. "Evolution of Online Campaigning: Increasing Interactivity in Candidate Web Sites and Blogs through Text and Technical Features." *Mass Communication and Society* 9 (1):21–44. doi: 10.1207/s15327825mcs0901_2.

Turnbull-Dugarte, S. J. 2019. "Selfies, Policies, or Votes? Political Party Use of Instagram in the 2015 and 2016 Spanish General Elections." *Social Media + Society* 1–15. doi: 10.1177/2056305119826129.

Vázquez-Herrero, J., S. Direito-Rebollal, and X. López-García. 2019. "Ephemeral Journalism: News Distribution Through Instagram Stories." *Social Media + Society.* doi: 10.1177/2056305119888657.

Vitak, J., and N. B. Ellison. 2013. "'There's a Network out There You Might as Well Tap': Exploring the Benefits of and Barriers to Exchanging Informational and Support-Based Resources on Facebook." *New Media & Society* 15 (2):243–59. doi: 10.1177/1461444812451566.

Wicks, R., and B. Souley. 2003. "Going Negative: Candidate Usage of Internet Web Sites during the 2000 Presidential Campaign." *Journalism & Mass Communication Quarterly* 80 (1):128–44. doi: 10.1177/107769900308000109.

Marketing Female Candidates as "Women": Gender and Partisanship's Influence on Issue Discussion on Twitter in 2020

Heather K. Evans

ABSTRACT

Previous work in the area of gender and social media has shown that women campaign and market themselves online very differently than men. While female candidates are more likely to discuss certain types of issues (like education and healthcare) in their campaigns, some research has shown that as more women are added to a congressional race, less attention is paid to those "women's issues." Given the steady increase in the number of women running for office and the increasing saliency of "women's issues" in American politics, this study examines the ways that female candidates marketed themselves differently than their male competitors in the 2020 U.S. House races on Twitter, paying particular attention to the influence of partisanship. The results show that women stressed different policy priorities in their tweets in 2020 compared to male candidates. While partisanship affects what issues get highlighted by candidates on Twitter, gender plays a role in whether candidates discuss issues that directly affect women as a group. Controlling for the context of the race, these findings demonstrate that when more women are added to a race, the likelihood of discussing "women's issues" increases.

As the dust settled on the 2020 election, many commentators reflected that this particular election-cycle represented a high-water mark for gender representation in the U.S. government. 120 women were elected to the U.S. House and 24 women to the U.S. Senate. This is a significant increase from even just a decade ago, when a total of only 90 women served in the House and Senate combined.

While this is a notable increase for female representation in the U.S. Congress, women still lag behind men in their overall representation, and in their likelihood of running for political office.[1] Women who do decide to run for seats in the U.S. Congress regularly state that there are gender biases present when they run, and that their decisions about whether to run and how to run are based partly on these biases. Some research shows that when women do decide to run, they do just as well as men in terms of how much money they raise and their likelihood of winning (Cook 1998; Fox 2013; Smith and Fox 2001; Hayes and Lawless 2016; Lawless and Pearson 2008). Yet, women are less likely to decide to run to begin with (Lawless 2015).

Common gender stereotypes and the belief that the political landscape will be biased against them contributes to many women deciding not to run (Hayes and Lawless 2016). Citizens regularly typecast female candidates as holding different personal characteristics than male candidates, and therefore are more likely to adequately deal with particular sets of issues that align with those stereotypes. Prior research shows that these stereotypes affect how women campaign and whether they stress "women's issues." Some have shown that women who stress "women's issues" in traditional campaigning methods receive a boost at the polls (Herrnson, Lay, and

Stokes 2003; Schaffner 2005), while other work shows that female candidates do not do as well if they run "as women" since voters believe they can only address those particular issues, while women may have greater success running on masculine issues (Larson 2001; Schneider 2014).

Most of the work that exists regarding how women market themselves and whether they address "women's issues" when they campaign centers around traditional advertising and media coverage. Political communication research is beginning to uncover the different ways that women use social media, however, given that this form of communication is attractive to "out-party" candidates (Karpf 2012). Evans and Clark (2016), for instance, show that female candidates who won seats to the U.S. House in 2012 were more likely to discuss "women's issues" on Twitter, and that this issue discussion was context-specific. The fewer women in the race, the more likely women would be to discuss "women's issues" to stand out from their competitors. Other work, however, has shown that while female candidates tweet more about "women's issues" in certain election years, the real differences in attention to particular issues is due to partisanship instead of gender (Hayes and Lawless 2016).

In this manuscript, I explore whether female candidates for the U.S. House in 2020 marketed themselves "as women" on Twitter by spending more time discussing "women's issues." Given the increase in the salience around non-economic issues, and the growth in the number of women both running for and winning election to the U.S. House, this investigation will give us a fuller picture regarding how female candidates market themselves on social media during their campaigns. In what follows, I explore three questions: (1) are female candidates more likely to talk about "women's issues" than male candidates on Twitter in 2020?, (2) how does partisanship play a role?, and finally (3) are candidates more likely to discuss "women's issues" in races with more women running for office?

Gender stereotypes, partisanship, and campaigning

Many scholars have argued that gender stereotypes affect whether women run for political office and how they campaign (Fox 1997; Herrnson and Lucas 2006; Kahn 1996; Kahn and Gordon 1997). Citizens regularly paint female candidates as being more caring and nurturing ("feminine" traits), while male candidates are stereotyped as being confident and strong ("masculine" traits) (Brown, Heighberger, and Shocket 1993; Leeper 1991; Rosenwasser and Seale 1988). These stereotypical characteristics of confidence and strength for male candidates and caring and compassion for female candidates lead citizens to view male candidates as being more competent in issue areas like foreign affairs and the economy, which are regularly referred to as "men's issues," and female candidates as being more able to handle issues like healthcare, education, and poverty, which are regularly referred to as "women's issues" (Huddy and Terkildsen 1993; Lawless 2004; Sanbonmatsu 2002; Brown, Heighberger, and Shocket 1993; Dolan 2010; Koch 1999).

These stereotypes can be very harmful to female candidates' campaigns, especially if they run in election years when "men's issues" are more salient than "women's issues." Female candidates, therefore, are in what many researchers have termed the "double-bind": they are seen as experts in these "women's issue" policy areas, so they could discuss these issues to appeal to voters, but if they do focus on these issues, they may be viewed as only able to deal with "women's issues." This is exactly what the research in this area has found. While some women who have campaigned as "women" have been helped at the polls, others have had no such luck (Herrnson, Lay, and Stokes 2003; Larson 2001; Bystrom et al. 2005; Dittmar 2015). Even in hypothetical situations, voters reward male candidates over female candidates when the issues at the front of the agenda are "men's issues" like terrorism and the economy (Falk and Kenski 2006). Similarly, other work has shown that women can be helped by emphasizing masculine stereotypes in their campaigns (Bauer 2018).

Since emphasizing "women's issues" can both help and harm female candidates' campaigns depending on the context of the election, there are reasons to expect women to discuss the same issues as their male competitors. As Lawless and Hayes (2016) argue, candidates should emphasize the issues that voters care the most about, which means that they should focus their campaigns on issues not specifically related to their gender. Instead of dividing on issues based on gender lines, if anything candidates should divide based on partisanship. Using campaign ads and messages on social media, Lawless and Hayes (2016) show that men and women in 2010 and 2014 ran nearly identical campaigns in terms of the issues they covered by partisanship. Dolan (2014) also finds in her analysis of campaign advertisements and candidate websites in 2010 that party mattered more in the selection of issues than gender.

Despite these previous findings regarding how gender affects the discussion of these issues regardless of partisanship, it is important for us to realize the connections that exist between partisanship and issue ownership in the United States. Within the U.S., issues traditionally described as "male," such as national security and defense, are historically owned by the Republicans, while more "feminine" issues, like education and healthcare, are owned by the Democrats (Egan 2013; Hayes 2005; Petrocik 1996). Because the parties pay significant attention to these "owned" issues, voters believe they are best equipped to deal with these issues when they become salient in the United States, and the party that is viewed as more proficient at dealing with those issues receives a gain at the ballot box (Budge and Farlie 1983; Petrocik 1996). Related to the work at hand with gendered issues among candidates on Twitter, there is a perception that Democrats should focus on Democratic or feminine issues, while Republicans should focus on Republican or masculine issues if they want to maximize marketing and strategy. This study's exploration about the effect of gender and campaigning on "women's issues" offers an opportunity to underscore the way that issue ownership might be limited in certain contexts and to see whether issue ownership persists in the face of gendered cross-pressures.

Additionally, other scholars have found significant differences in the issues that candidates discuss both in person and online, even when controlling for partisanship which again might signal a limit of issue ownership on gendered campaigning on certain issues. Evans and Clark (2016) find in their analysis of tweets sent by candidates running for the U.S. House in 2012 that women are more likely to campaign as "outsiders." Women in 2012 were more likely to talk about general issues in their tweets, and when Evans and Clark separate out "women's issues" from the rest, they find that women were significantly more likely to discuss these topics, even when controlling for partisanship. Schaffner (2005) and Debelko and Herrnson (1997) also find that Democratic women are more likely to traditionally campaign on "women's issues" like healthcare and abortion than Democratic men, and the same is true for Republican women compared to Republican men. Herrick (2016) also shows in her analysis of state legislative websites in 2012 that female candidates are more likely to campaign on "women's issues" regardless of partisanship.

All of these findings suggest that female candidates have to consider more strategic elements to their campaigns when they decide to run for office. Wagner, Gainous, and Holman (2017) state that "women face and perceive a gendered disadvantage when seeking office, which may translate into various strategic campaigning," which results in female candidates not only being early and frequent users of social media like Twitter, but also in the content of the tweets they send (Evans and Clark 2016).

Research questions

The research cited above examining gender and online campaigning is a bit dated and contradictory. Both Evans and Clark (2016) and Hayes and Lawless (2016) examine some of the earliest elections when candidates used Twitter for campaign purposes (2010, 2012, 2014). As a recent report from Pew Research reveals, members of Congress tweet nearly twice as often as they even did four years ago, have nearly three times as many followers, and receive nearly six times as many retweets (Kessel et al. 2020). Furthermore, there has been a significant increase in the number of women running for office since 2014, and growth in the salience of "women's issues" for the American public.

Given the shifts in the types of candidates running for congressional office and the increase in their use of Twitter, in what follows I explore whether female candidates today on Twitter market themselves differently in terms of the issues they discuss. Are female candidates more likely to discuss "women's issues" or "men's issues" than their male counterparts, or do they campaign on Twitter in similar ways? Since other scholars have shown that partisanship affects issue discussion more than gender and for the persistence of issue ownership connections among the two U.S. parties, I test for their cumulative effects. Finally, as Evans and Clark (2016) established in their work on the 2012 election, I want to follow up on the effect of adding more women to congressional races. When more women run, does the discussion surrounding "women's issues" increase? I anticipate that the nature of the 2020 election with the high number of female candidates will lead women to focus more on women's issues more frequently on Twitter in their campaign marketing than their male counterparts, but that these effects might be affected by partisanship as well. I hypothesize that women will focus more on women's issues irrespective of partisanship, but that variation among women will be affected by partisan inclinations.

Method

Using a dataset of all tweets sent by all candidates for the U.S. House during the last two months of the election, I am able to investigate whether women marketed themselves differently on Twitter than men did in 2020.[2] Collecting these tweets for the two months prior to the election allows me to compare my results to earlier work in this area and is the time when almost all state primary elections have concluded. First, with the help of an undergraduate student at my college and two graduate students at other colleges in the U.S., we collected the names, party identification, and gender of each of candidates in all U.S. House races using Ballotpedia.org, including major and minor party candidates (Republicans, Democrats, and third-party candidates). In total, we collected demographic information for 1,130 candidates. We also collected the campaign Twitter IDs for each candidate.[3] In total, we collected 216,231 tweets, retweets, and replies. Since I am interested in information that the candidate pushed themselves (and not just amplified from other sources), this analysis focuses only on tweets and replies. When retweets are dropped from this dataset, 147,799 tweets remain for a total of 736 candidates (472 male candidates and 264 female candidates). The final dataset includes tweets for 316 Republicans, 367 Democrats, and 53 third-party candidates.[4]

To determine what issues candidates were focusing on in 2020, I did a key word/phrase search using Stata. Following in the footsteps of Evans and Clark (2016), I searched for statements about "women's issues" and "men's issues." When it comes to defining "women's issues," previous scholars have included core issues that have traditionally been associated with women, like health and education, while other scholars have merged issues like equal rights and feminist issues into a broader definition of "women's issues" (Bratton 2002; Dodson and Carroll 1991; Swers 2002; Wolbrecht 2000; Herring 2016). Like Evans and Clark (2016), I searched for issues that "directly and disproportionately affect women as a group," including traditional issues like healthcare, welfare, education, the environment, children, and family, as well as feminist concerns that "seek to improve the social, economic, and political status of women as a group." I also include crimes that disproportionately affect women as a group, and specific healthcare concerns. I deleted some issues that were specific to the 2012 race from the Evans and Clark (2016) codebook, and included additional key words and phrases for 2020: glass ceiling, sexual harassment, bullying, #MeToo, and #TimesUp. I also coded for "men's issues" by searching for the list of key words and phrases that were included in Evans and Clark (2016) and Evans (2016), with some slight election year specific adjustments. A full list of the words and phrases used in my analysis is given in Table 1. Part of the analysis that follows involves a count of the number of tweets that include the words and phrases in Table 1 that fit each of these different topics (like the number of tweets about healthcare and the economy), while at other times I use a cumulative total number of tweets that fit under "women's issues" and "men's issues." If a tweet

Table 1. Gendered issues on Twitter – words and phrases.

Women's Issues	Men's Issues
Bullying	Agriculture/farm
Childcare/child care/daycare	Economy/business/deficit/debt/taxes/budget/ spending
Domestic violence/sexual assault/domestic abuse/rape/rapist	
Education/college/school	Guns
Equality/discrimination	Homeland security/ 9/11
Family/families	Immigration/border/amnesty
Food stamps/SNAP	International relations/foreign affairs/war/ Iraq/ Afghanistan/Syria/Benghazi/Russia/ China/NATO
Gay marriage/LGBT/#LoveisLove	
Glass Ceiling	Liberty
Healthcare/Health care/ACA/Affordable Care Act/Obamacare	Marijuana/legalization/pot/weed
Medicare/Medicaid	
Poverty/poor	
Sexual harassment/#MeToo /#TimesUp	
Social Security/SS/SSA/	
SSDC/SSDI/Social assistance	
Welfare	
WIC/children/youth/kids/adolescent	
Woman/women/female/girl	
Women's Health Care: Abortion/ pro-choice/pro-life	
Birth control/ Plan B/ contraception/ reproductive/ Planned Parenthood	

mentioned both healthcare and the economy, it was coded as both a healthcare tweet and an economy tweet, and then was also used in the counts for both "women's issues" and "men's issues."

Findings

During the final two months of the 2020 election, candidates for the U.S. House sent an average of 200 tweets and replies. Female candidates sent significantly more tweets than male candidates (women sent 243 tweets, men sent 177 tweets on average, comparison of means t-test, $p = 0.0116$). When I examine the number of tweets by partisanship over those last two months, I find that Democrats and third-party candidates tweeted the most (Democrats = 226; Third Party = 224; Republicans = 166).[5]

After searching each tweet for whether the statement referenced any men's or women's issues, I then created two cumulative variables, one for overall "women's issues" and one for "men's issues." During the 2020 election, there was more conversation surrounding "women's issues" than "men's issues." My data reveal that on average, "women's issues" were discussed 38.5 times, compared to 20.7 times for "men's issues."

Figure 1 shows the distribution of issue discussion across all of the issues included. As the figure indicates, some of the issues and topics were not discussed regularly by candidates in 2020, while others were. "Women's issues" that were discussed most often were healthcare, family, women, and education. Tweets about WIC (which includes tweets about "children" and "kids") and Medicare were also common. In terms of "men's issues," the leading topics were those about the economy (business, taxes, spending) and international relations.

Table 2 presents the candidates who tweeted most often about these issues. In terms of "women's issues," each candidate included these words and phrases in their tweets over 300 times. The candidate who tweeted the most about topics related to "women's issues" was Christine Alexandria Olivo, an independent candidate running in the 24th district of Florida (869 times). The prolific tweeters in the second column mentioned "men's issues" at least 200 times, with the most comments about these topics coming from Nate McMurray, a Democratic candidate from New York's 27th district (at 332 times).

Table 2 demonstrates that at least among the prolific tweeters, the group discussing "women's issues" is dominated by Democrats and third-party candidates. No Republican candidate made

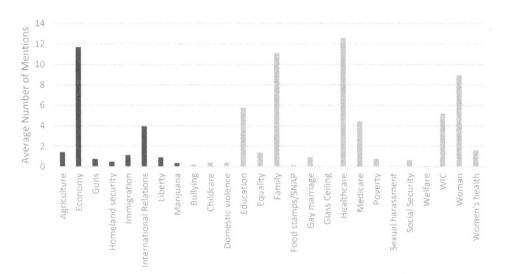

Figure 1. Issue mentions on Twitter in 2020.

Table 2. Prolific women's and men's issue Tweeters in 2020.

Women's Issues	Men's Issues
Christine Alexandria Olivo (I)	Nate McMurray (D)
Mia Mason (D)	Kim Mangone (D)
Nate McMurray (D)	Joe Evans (L)
Christopher Hale (D)	Elise Stefanik (R)
Harry Burger (G)	Buzz Patterson (R)
Lindsey Simmons (D)	Mia Mason (D)

D = Democrat, R = Republican, I = Independent, G = Green Party, L = Libertarian.

the top list. When it comes to "men's issues" however, Democrats, Republicans, and third-party candidates are included.

To get a better sense of how gender is related to issue discussion, I divided my list of candidates by gender. Women sent approximately 55.9 tweets about "women's issues," and 23.4 tweets about "men's issues," on average. Men, on the other hand, sent 28.9 tweets about "women's issues" and 19.3 tweets about "men's issues" on average. This means that women sent more tweets that addressed all of these issues than men. A difference of means t-test reveals that women sent significantly more tweets about "women's issues," while the difference between them on "men's issues" was not significant (for "women's issues", $p < 0.0001$; for "men's issues", $p = 0.11$).

As some have argued (Hayes and Lawless 2016), these differences might be the product of partisanship and conversations around issue ownership instead of gender. To explore whether this is the case, I first compared the differences of means between the four groups (Democratic women, Democratic men, Republican women, and Republican men). As Figure 2 demonstrates, female candidates tweet more about all of these topics than men do, in each partisanship pair. Democratic women lead the way in terms of discussion of "women's issues," but Republican women lead for "men's issues." Democratic men tweet a few more times than Republican women about "women's issues," while Republican men send the fewest tweets about these topics.[6]

To see the cumulative effect of gender and partisanship, I estimated four negative binomial regression models since my dependent variable is a count and to account for overdispersion in the data. The dependent variable is the count of the number of words used by candidates for "female issues" and "male issues." The three main independent variables are the interaction effects for gender and partisanship, excluding third party candidates. Since we should also consider the number of tweets and not just their frequency, I also control for the number of tweets sent by each candidate ("total tweets") in the last two models. The odds ratios are displayed in Table 3

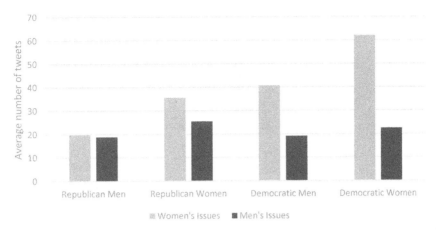

Figure 2. Gender, partisanship, and issue discussion.

Table 3. Negative binomial regression models for Tweets about "women's issues" and "men's issues".

	Women's Issues		Men's Issues	
Gendered Partisanship				
Democratic Female	3.12 (0.37)**	2.74 (0.27)**	1.19 (0.15)	0.90 (0.09)
Republican Female	1.79 (0.28)**	1.48 (0.19)**	1.34 (0.22)+	1.04 (0.14)
Democratic Male	2.04 (0.24)**	1.67 (0.16)**	1.01 (0.13)	0.78 (0.07)*
Total Tweets	--------	1.003 (0.00)**	--------	1.003 (0.00)**
_cons	19.88 (1.58)**	8.49 (0.64)**	18.96 (1.57)**	8.65 (0.65)**
Pseudo R2	0.01	0.07	0.00	0.06

Note: Cells present the Odds Ratios. Standard errors given in parentheses.
Baseline category for Gender x Partisanship variable is Republican Men.
**p ≤ 0.01, *p ≤ 0.05, + p ≤ 0.10.

for ease of interpretation. These results show that when it comes to mentioning "female issues," women are significantly more likely to do so even after controlling for partisanship and the overall activity of candidates on Twitter. Holding all variables at their means, the first column shows that Republican women sent 1.79 times as many tweets than Republican men about "women's issues." Democratic men and Democratic women are also more likely to tweet about "women's issues," with Democratic women leading the way by sending over three times as many tweets about these topics than Republican men. The second column of Table 3 also reveals that even when we control for the number of tweets being sent by these candidates, these three groups continue to out-tweet Republican men about "women's issues." The expected increase in the number of "women's issues" being discussed by Democratic men compared to Republican men is 67%, while the increase is 49% for Republican women compared to Republican men. Finally, Democratic women continue to hold a sizeable lead over Republican men, sending 2.74 times as many tweets about these topics.

When we turn our attention to tweeting about "men's issues," we see that there are very few significant differences between the groups. First, when examining the third column, I find that Republican women are the only group that approaches significance when compared to Republican men. Republican women send approximately 34% more tweets about "men's issues" than Republican men. However, my results in the last column of Table 3 show that once the total number of tweets is included, female candidates are not more likely to send tweets about these topics than Republican men (no matter their partisanship). The only variable that is significant is the result for Democratic men, which demonstrates that Democratic men send significantly fewer tweets about these topics than Republican men, holding all other variables at their means.

I would also like to note that for both the second and fourth columns of Table 3, those who tweet more often were also more likely to tweet about these topics. Each additional tweet a

Table 4. Negative binomial regression models for Tweets about "women's issues" and "men's issues".

	Women's Issues	Men's Issues
Female	1.41 (0.15)**	0.96 (0.11)
Republican	.61 (0.05)**	1.25 (0.10)**
Total % Women	1.46 (0.25)*	1.43 (0.25)*
Total Tweets	1.003 (0.00)**	1.003 (0.00)**
_cons	12.45 (0.99)**	6.25 (0.50)**
Pseudo R2	0.07	0.07

Note: Cells present the Odds Ratios. Standard errors given in parentheses.
**$p \leq 0.01$, *$p \leq 0.05$.

candidate sent produced a .3% increase in the number of tweets about "women's issues" and "men's issues."

Overall these results paint an interesting picture regarding the ways that female candidates marketed themselves differently than male candidates during the 2020 election. Women were more likely to include references to policy issues than men, but when partisanship and the total number of tweets sent are controlled for, I find that female candidates are not more likely to tweet about "men's issues." As I hypothesized, female candidates are significantly more likely to discuss "women's issues" than male candidates regardless of partisanship.

As some earlier research in the area of gender and online campaigning has found, the likelihood of female candidates discussing "women's issues" may differ in terms of the characteristics of the race in which they find themselves. If there is only one female in the race, there may be a greater likelihood of that particular female candidate spending more time on "women's issues" so that she can stand apart from her male competitors, and campaign on something that she is already typecast into being more of an expert on. Evans and Clark (2016) argue that when women square off against other female candidates, they become less likely to market themselves as "female" candidates by discussing these so-called "women's issues" because they share policy expertise with their challengers.

To see whether their status in the race affects whether they discuss these policy issues, I calculated two additional negative binomial regression models. My independent variables are again the number of times candidates mentioned "women's issues" or "men's issues" during the last two months of the election. Instead of breaking apart my groups by gender and partisanship, I control for gender and partisanship as dummy variables (scored 1 for female and 1 for Republican, 0 otherwise), the total number of tweets sent, and the percentage of female candidates in each race. My odds-ratio results are displayed in Table 4.

Both gender and the percentage of women in the race has a large effect on whether a candidate discusses "women's issues," with women sending 1.4 times as many tweets about these issues. Candidates in all female-candidate races are predicted to send 1.46 times as many tweets about "women's issues" than those in races with no women running. Republicans send 40% fewer tweets about these issues. Like my earlier results, those who tweet more often are slightly more likely to discuss "women's issues."

When it comes to discussing "men's issues," these results show that gender does not have an effect when including these additional variables, but adding women to the race has a positive and significant effect. Races with an all-female ticket send approximately 1.43 times as many tweets about "men's issues" as those with no women running. Partisanship is significant in this model, with Republicans sending more tweets about "men's issues," and those who tweet more often are more likely to mention these issues as well.

The results presented in Table 4 stand in contrast to the work by Evans and Clark (2016). In their work on the 2012 election, Evans and Clark show that as the percentage of females in a race increases, there is no discernable impact on the likelihood of tweeting about women's issues. They do, however, find that adding women to a race increases issue discussion overall. While I find here that adding women to the race does have a significant impact on discussing "men's issues," I also find that it increases discussion about "women's issues."

The reasons I find a significant difference for "women's issues" here compared to the early work by Evans and Clark are two-fold. First, Evans and Clark's work on the 2012 election only incorporates tweets sent by candidates who won seats in the U.S. House, not those who also lost. This means that they had significantly fewer female candidates in their analysis (N = 78 women). My analysis incorporates all candidates who ran in 2020, whether they won or lost (N = 264 women).

Secondly, there was less issue discussion overall in 2012 about "women's issues" than in 2020. In the 2012 data, the mean number of "women's issues" tweets was 4.23. In 2020, the mean number of "women's issues" per candidate was 38.58. In 2012, 190 candidates did not mention "women's issues" at all. In 2020, only 57 candidates never mentioned these topics.

Conclusion

Female representation in the U.S. Congress has increased steadily over the past 20 years. The last three elections have produced the largest growth thus far in gender representation in the U.S. House and Senate. In 2016, the highest number of women ever ran for the U.S. Senate, at 40. Similarly, 272 women ran for seats in the House of Representatives with 167 winning their primaries, beating the prior record set in 2012 (The Center for American Women and Politics). That year, 85 women won seats in the House while 20 won seats in the Senate (19.6% of total congressional seats). Continuing that trend, during the 2018 elections, we saw a significant increase in the number of women running. There was a 20% increase in the number of women elected to seats in Congress (101 Representatives, 25 Senators, or 23.5% of total congressional seats). By all means, one could argue that 2018 was truly the "Year of the Woman." But then came 2020. After Republican women suffered loses in 2018, they borrowed a page from their Democratic colleagues and focused on running women for Congress in 2020. Republican women flipped many districts in 2020, taking 35 U.S. House seats —a historical high-water mark for Republicans. In total, we now have a U.S. House and Senate that is more representative of the U.S. population than ever before (in terms of gender), with 144 women elected to Congress, 120 women to the U.S. House and 24 women to the U.S. Senate (27% of total congressional seats).

Did these newly elected women focus on issues during their elections that were different than their male counterparts? Earlier research on this topic has been mixed, with some scholars finding significant differences between men and women in terms of their issue discussions, and others finding that partisanship was key. In the analysis presented here, I show that women were significantly more likely to talk about "women's issues" on Twitter than men regardless of partisanship. Both Republican and Democratic women were more likely to talk about "women's issues," and when more women were added to the race, the likelihood of discussing "women's issues" increased.

One of the limitations to this line research is that the list of "women's issues" and "men's issues" is constantly changing and evolving, and the list used here is not exhaustive. With each new election comes new important issues. Other issues, like energy, crime, and infrastructure, could be incorporated into future work on issue-discussion. Some of these topics, however, like energy and infrastructure, do not fit cleanly into one gendered-issue type. During the 2020 election, citizens said that the three top issues for them were COVID-19, the economy, and race relations.[7] I did not include any codes here for issues related to racial justice, like tweets about Black Lives Matter or defunding the police, but some work suggests that these topics were ignored by U.S. congressional candidates in 2020 (Evans and Moore 2020). Civil rights are typically categorized as "women's issues" (Herrick 2016), so future work regarding the 2020 congressional elections should examine whether tweets about Black Lives Matter were more prevalent in female candidates' tweets.

Future work should also explore whether the marketing of female candidates as "women" by focusing on "women's issues" was occurring in other forms of candidate communication and whether the presence of more women in a race affected their issue discussion. Were women more likely to discuss "women's issues" in campaign ads as well? Research from the Political Advertising Resource Center of the Rosenker Center for Political Communication and Civic Leadership at the University of Maryland shows that women who ran in 2018 sidestepped issues like equal pay and abortion access. Instead of focusing on "women's issues" in 2018, researchers found that among the 25 female candidates in their study women instead were very cautious and produced ads that portrayed them as being "tough" (Parry-Giles et al. 2019). Whether that was the case in 2020 has yet to be uncovered, and furthermore, this research only explores a subset of female candidates and does not examine the effect of additional women in the race.

Finally, while these findings show that women are more likely to talk about these issues on the campaign trail on Twitter, do they work on those issues when they get in office? Other scholarship has shown that once women win, they legislate differently. Women are more likely to focus on "women's issues" like equal pay and reproductive rights when they replace men from the same districts (Gerrity, Osborn, and Mendez 2007), and women from both sides of the aisle are more likely to sponsor and co-sponsor legislation dealing with women's issues (Swers 2002). Given these findings, we should expect that the new U.S. Congress will sponsor more bills dealing with "women's issues" than any Congress that has come before.

Notes

1. Women serve in approximately 27% of all seats in the U.S. Congress.
2. I'd like to thank Mark Willis at ProPublica for his assistance in gathering these tweets. These tweets were collected using the Twitter API.
3. I'd like to thank Rian Moore for his assistance in the summer of 2020 in collecting this information for 30 of these states. The other twenty states were divided between two graduate research assistants of two of my colleagues, Annelise Russell and Bryan Gervais.
4. Many third-party candidates did not have a Twitter account.
5. The difference between Democrats and Republicans is also significant. Using a difference of means t-test – comparing Democrats to Republicans: $p = 0.0168$; comparing third-party candidates to Republicans: $p = 0.2209$.
6. When examining issue discussion by third-party candidates, I also find that women lead the way as well, although that is to be expected given that the most prolific tweeter was a female independent candidate. There are so few female third-party candidates in my dataset (9) that it is difficult to say much about that data broken down by gender.
7. https://news.gallup.com/poll/1675/most-important-problem.aspx

References

Bauer, Nichole M. 2018. "Untangling the relationship between partisanship, gender stereotypes, and support for female candidates." *Journal of Women, Politics & Policy* 39 (1):1–25.

Bratton, Kathleen A. 2002. "The Effect of Legislative Diversity on Agenda Setting: Evidence from Six State Legislatures." *American Politics Research* 30 (2):115–42. doi: 10.1177/1532673X02030002001.

Brown, Clyde, Neil R. Heighberger, and Peter A. Shocket. 1993. "Gender-Based Differences in Perceptions of Male and Female City Council Candidates." *Women & Politics* 13 (1):1–17. doi: 10.1300/J014v13n01_01.

Budge, Ian, and Dennis J. Farlie. 1983. *Explaining and Predicting Elections: Issue Effects and Party Strategies in Twenty-Three Democracies*. London: Unwin Hyman.

Bystrom, Dianne G., Terry Robertson, Mary Christine Banwart, and Lynda Lee Kaid. 2005. Gender and candidate communication: Videostyle, webstyle, newstyle. Routledge.

Cook, Elizabeth Adell. 1998. "Voter Reaction to Women Candidates." In *Women and Elective Office*, edited by Sue Thomas and Clyde Wilcox (pp. 56–72). New York: Oxford University Press.

Dittmar, Kelly. 2015. "Encouragement is not enough: Addressing social and structural barriers to female recruitment." *Politics & Gender* 11 (4):759–765.

Dodson, Debra L., and Susan J. Carroll. 1991. "Reshaping the Agenda: Women in State Legislatures." Center for the American Woman and Politics, New Brunswick, NJ. https://cawp.rutgers.edu/reshaping-agenda-women-state-legislatures

Dolan, Kathleen. 2010. "The Impact of Gendered Stereotyped Evaluations on Support for Women Candidates." *Political Behavior* 32 (1):69–88. doi: 10.1007/s11109-009-9090-4.

Dolan, Kathleen. 2014. *When Does Gender Matter? Women Candidates and Gender Stereotypes in American Elections*. New York: Oxford University Press.

Egan, Patrick J. 2013. *Partisan Priorities: How Issue Ownership Drives and Distorts American Politics*. New York: Cambridge University Press.

Evans, Heather K. 2016. "Do Women Only Talk about "Female Issues"? Gender and Issue Discussion on Twitter." *Online Information Review* 40 (5):660–72. doi: 10.1108/OIR-10-2015-0338.

Evans, Heather K, and Jennifer Hayes Clark. 2016. ""You Tweet like a Girl!": How Female Candidates Campaign on Twitter." *American Politics Research* 44 (2):326–52. doi: 10.1177/1532673X15597747.

Evans, Heather K., and Rian F Moore. 2020. "Did the Economy, COVID-19, or Black Lives Matter to the Senate Candidates in 2020?" U.S. Election Analysis 2020: Media, Voters, and the Campaign. https://www.electionanalysis.ws/us/president2020/section-5-social-media/did-the-economy-covid-19-or-black-lives-matter-to-th e-senate-candidates-in-2020/

Fox, Richard. 1997. *Gender Dynamics in Congressional Elections*. Thousand Oaks, CA: SAGE.

Fox, Richard. 2013. "Congressional Elections: Women's Candidacies and the Road to Gender Parity." In *Gender and Elections*. 3rd ed., edited by Susan J. Carroll and Richard L. Fox (pp. 190–210). New York: Cambridge University Press.

Gerrity, Jessica, Tracy Osborn, and Jeanette Morehouse Mendez. 2007. "Women and Representation: A Different View of the District?" *Politics & Gender* 3 (02):179–200. doi: 10.1017/S1743923X07000025.

Hayes, Danny. 2005. "Candidate Qualities through a Partisan Lens: A Theory of Trait Ownership." *American Journal of Political Science* 49 (4):908–23. doi: 10.1111/j.1540-5907.2005.00163.x.

Hayes, Danny, and Jennifer L. Lawless. 2016. *Women on the Run: Gender, Media, and Political Campaigning in a Polarized Era*. New York: Cambridge University Press.

Herrick, Rebekah. 2016. "Gender Themes in State Legislative Candidates' Websites." *The Social Science Journal* 53 (3):282–90. doi: 10.1016/j.soscij.2016.05.001.

Herrnson, Paul S. J. Celeste Lay, and A.K. Stokes. 2003. "Women running 'as women': Candidate gender, campaign issues, and votetargeting strategies." *The Journal of Politics* 65:244–55.

Herrnson, Paul S, and Jennifer C. Lucas. 2006. "The Fairer Sex? Gender and Negative Campaigning in U.S. Elections." *American Politics Research* 34 (1):69–94. doi: 10.1177/1532673X05278038.

Huddy, Leonie, and Nayda Terkildsen. 1993. "Gender Stereotypes and the Perception of Male and Female Candidates." *American Journal of Political Science* 37 (1):119–47. doi: 10.2307/2111526.

Kahn, Kim Fridkin. 1996. *The Political Consequences of Being a Woman*. New York: Columbia University Press.

Kahn, Kim Fridkin, and Ann Gordon. 1997. "How Women Campaign for the U.S. Senate: Substance and Strategy." In *Women, Media, and Politics*, edited by P. Norris, 59–76. New York: Oxford University Press.

Karpf, David. 2012. *The Move-On Effect*. New York: Oxford University Press.

Kessel, PatrickVan, Regina Widjaya, Sono Shah, Arron Smith, and Adam Hughes. 2020. "Congress Soars to New Heights on Social Media." *Pew Research Center*, July 16. https://www.pewresearch.org/internet/2020/07/16/congress-soars-to-new-heights-on-social-media/

Koch, JeffreyW. 1999. "Candidate Gender and Assessments of Senate Candidates." *Social Science Quarterly* 80: 84–96. https://www.jstor.org/stable/42863875

La Cour Dabelko, Kirsten, and Paul S. Herrnson. 1997. "Women's and Men's Campaigns for the US House of Representatives." *Political Research Quarterly* 50 (1):121–135.

Larson, Stephanie Greco. 2001. ""Running as Women"? A Comparison of Female and Male Pennsylvania Assembly Candidates' Campaign Brochures." *Women & Politics* 22 (2):107–124.

Lawless, Jennifer L. 2004. "Women, War, and Winning Elections: Gender Stereotyping in the Post September 11th Era." *Political Research Quarterly* 57 (3):479–90. doi: 10.2307/3219857.

Lawless, Jennifer L. 2015. "Female Candidates and Legislators." *Annual Review of Political Science* 18 (1):349–66. doi: 10.1146/annurev-polisci-020614-094613.

Lawless, Jennifer L, and Kathryn Pearson. 2008. "The Primary Reason for Women's under-Representation: Re-Evaluating the Convention Wisdom." *The Journal of Politics* 70 (1):67–82. doi: 10.1017/S002238160708005X.

Leeper, Mark. 1991. "The Impact of Prejudice on Female Candidates: An Experimental Look at Voter Inference." *American Politics Quarterly* 19 (2):248–61. doi: 10.1177/1532673X9101900206.

Parry-Giles, Shawn, Aya Hussein Farhat, Matthew Salzano, and Skyede Saint Felix. 2019. "Women Who Ran for Congress Avoided Women's Issues in Their Campaign Ads." *The Conversation*. https://theconversation.com/women-who-ran-for-congress-avoided-womens-issues-in-their-campaign-ads-109211

Petrocik, John R. 1996. "Issue Ownership in Presidential Elections, with a 1980 Case Study." *American Journal of Political Science* 40 (3):825–50. doi: 10.2307/2111797.

Rosenwasser, Shirley M., and Jana Seale. 1988. "Attitudes toward a Hypothetical Male or Female Presidential Candidate: A Research Note." *Political Psychology* 9 (4):591–8. doi: 10.2307/3791529.

Sanbonmatsu, Kira. 2002. "Gender Stereotypes and Vote Choice." *American Journal of Political Science* 46 (1):20–34. doi: 10.2307/3088412.

Schaffner, Brian F. 2005. "Priming Gender: Campaigning on Women's Issues in U.S. Senate Elections." *American Journal of Political Science* 49 (4):803–17. doi: 10.1111/j.1540-5907.2005.00156.x.

Schneider, Monica C. 2014. "The Effects of Gender-Bending on Candidate Evaluations." *Journal of Women, Politics, and Policy* 35 (1):55–77. doi: 10.1080/1554477X.2014.863697.

Smith, Eric R. A. N., and Richard L. Fox. 2001. "A Research Note: The Electoral Fortunes of Women Candidates for Congress." *Political Research Quarterly* 54 (1):205–21. doi: 10.2307/449215.

Swers, Michelle L. 2002. *The Difference Women Make*. Chicago, IL: University of Chicago Press.

Wagner, Kevin M., Jason Gainous, and Mirya R. Holman. 2017. "I Am Woman, Hear Me Tweet! Gender Differences in Twitter Use among Congressional Candidates." *Journal of Women, Politics, and Policy* 38 (4):430–55. doi: 10.1080/1554477X.2016.1268871.

Wolbrecht, Christina. 2000. *The Politics of Women's Rights: Parties, Positions, and Change*. Princeton, NJ: Princeton University Press.

Tipping the Twitter vs. News Media Scale? Conducting a Third Assessment of Intermedia Agenda-Setting Effects during the Presidential Nomination Season

Bethany Anne Conway, Eric Tsetsi, Kate Kenski, and Yotam Shmargad

ABSTRACT
Two previous studies investigated the relationship between newspaper issue agendas and those of candidate and campaign Twitter feeds during the presidential nomination season in 2012 and 2016. Both found the intermedia agenda-setting power resided with newspapers. This study replicates the previous two by examining the issue agendas of the nation's top newspapers and those of candidate and campaign Twitter feeds during the 2020 presidential nomination season. Computer-assisted content analysis and time-series analysis suggest that intermedia agenda-setting power was more even-handed during the 2020 nomination seasons compared to 2012 and 2016, although this finding depends on the metric used.

On January 8, 2021, two days after an angry mob stormed the U.S. Capitol in Washington, D.C., Twitter permanently banned President Donald Trump's social media account (McClusky and Zennie 2021). This was not the first time that Twitter blocked the president. The company placed fact-check warning labels on President Trump countless times and suspended his use of the platform for 12 hours on the previous day (Clayton, Kelion, and Molloy 2021). While it was Twitter's legal right to take such action, the ban sent a powerful message about his use of the platform—that Twitter provided Trump with the power to sway public opinion and behavior. By choosing to emphasize certain issues over others on Twitter, Trump had the ability to build public agendas.

Such potential to influence opinions is not confined to the public. Research suggests Twitter use by politicians can influence what traditional media outlets choose to cover (Conway, Kenski, and Wang 2015; Conway et al. 2018; Jungherr 2016; Kenski and Conway 2016; Sayre et al. 2010; Shapiro and Hemphill 2017; Stromer-Galley 2014; Wells et al. 2016). The role news media played in perpetuating Trump's "Twitter power" by citing his tweets and, thus, repeating his claims, continues to draw attention. We investigate how powerful this relationship was during the 2020 nomination season. Politicians try to harness the power of social media to set news media agendas (Bimber 2014; Groshek and Groshek 2013; Meraz 2009; Kreiss 2016, 2016; Parmelee 2013a), but this relationship should be described as reciprocal—meaning that predictive power resides with both social media and traditional news media (Conway, Kenski, and Wang 2015; Kenski and Jamieson 2017; Sayre et al. 2010). The magnitude of these relationships also varies depending on the issue in question (Conway, Kenski, and Wang 2015; Conway et al. 2018) and the time lag used in a given analysis (Harder, Sevenans, and Van Aelst 2017; Shapiro and Hemphill 2017).

One particular case where there is some question about the influence of Twitter use on news media coverage is during the presidential nomination season. In two studies of issue emphasis during the presidential nomination season, Conway, Kenski, and Wang (2015) and Conway et al. (2018) found that newspapers exhibited greater influence on candidate Twitter feeds than the reverse. Casual arguments for such findings include (1) newspapers set the agenda for television (Roberts and McCombs 1994), increasing their agenda-setting power; (2) citing newspaper coverage offers a degree of legitimation (Conway, Kenski, and Wang 2015; Harder, Sevenans, and Van Aelst 2017); (3) issue emphasis may be infrequent during nomination campaigns in general, as politicians try to maintain a level of ambiguity (Kendall 2016); and (4) Trump's tweets often fail to focus on important issues (Kopan 2016). Yet no president before Trump used Twitter with such frequency to spread such incendiary—and attention-grabbing—rhetoric (Quealy 2021).

Here, we replicate two previous studies (Conway, Kenski, and Wang 2015; Conway et al. 2018), examining whether Trump tipped the scale of intermedia agenda-setting power toward Twitter during the 2020 presidential nomination season. Such research is pertinent as we continue to scrutinize the role of social media in the agenda-setting process (Bennett and Iyengar 2008; Groshek and Groshek 2013; Harder, Sevenans, and Van Aelst 2017; Kreiss 2016; Towner and Dulio 2012; Van Aelst et al. 2017). Our results suggest that at least in 2020 Twitter matched newspapers in predictive power. After four election cycles where Twitter's role in politics has continued to shift, predictions about the loss of gatekeeping influence among traditional media are gaining traction (Bennett and Iyengar 2008).

The News-Media-to-Twitter Relationship

Candidates have always made strategic decisions regarding their correspondence with news media and the public (Bendle 2014). Such communication, especially within social media, is perhaps most dynamic during the nomination season as candidates jockey for position and try to gain political momentum (Ryoo and Bendle 2017). In this study, we analyzed the impact of social media marketing on behalf of candidates and campaigns on the news media agenda. We do this through the lens of intermedia agenda setting, which focuses on how different media drive one another's content (Denham 2010; McCombs 2004; Weaver and Choi 2014). In the past, this research focused on campaign information in the form of press releases, advertisements, websites, and blogs (Boyle 2001; Dunn 2009; Lancendorfer and Lee 2010; Lopez-Escobar et al. 1998; Sweetser, Golan, and Wanta 2008). Today, much research focuses on social media use on behalf of politicians and parties (Conway, Kenski, and Wang 2015; Conway et al. 2018; Jacobson 2013; Jungherr 2016; Meraz 2009; Sayre et al. 2010), a force that became integral to the campaign scene little more than a decade ago. Twitter specifically is essential to political campaigns (Kapko 2016; Shmargad and Sanchez 2022). It is fair to say that, at least with regard to politics, social media have surpassed previous campaign materials when it comes to reaching journalists both in frequency and in power.

Journalists actively use Twitter to source and build stories just as they did with former information subsidies (Farhi 2009; Parmelee 2013a, 2013b). Recent work suggests journalists even liken Twitter to a news wire (Lawrence 2015) that allows them to do work without true "mobilization" (Lecheler and Kruikemeier 2016). Content analyses also suggest journalists "use Twitter quotes to cite official sources more than non-official sources" (Bane 2019: 199). Overall, journalists have "adopted an opportunistic model, tapping social media to fulfill a need for information until professional journalists [arrive] on the scene, hours or even days later" (Hermida 2012: 664).

Though politicians can use Twitter as a megaphone to build the press' agenda, this does not guarantee they are successful. Research on the agenda-building relationship shows "candidates and newspapers can exert mutual influence on each other" (Lancendorfer and Lee 2010: 201). Previous studies show traditional news media outlets often set the Twitter agenda when it comes to various events, crises or otherwise (Ceron, Curini, and Iacus 2016; Rogstad 2016; Su and Borah 2019; Vargo, Basilaia, and Shaw 2015). Moreover, when it comes to debates on social media, politicians "are highly dependent on the media infrastructure," in that they rely on mainstream media brands to provide evidence for their claims (Enli and Simonsen 2018: 1091). This top-down conceptualization of the news-media-to-Twitter agenda has much support. Pertinent to the current study, in the case of the 2012 nomination season, Conway, Kenski, and Wang (2015) used time series analysis to examine whether the top U.S. newspapers predicted candidate and party issue emphasis on Twitter, focusing on eight issues. They found that newspaper issue emphasis predicted Twitter issue emphasis to a greater extent than the reverse both in terms of the numbers of leads and their strength. Later, during the 2016 nomination season, Conway et al. (2018) once again found that those same newspapers out predicted Twitter both overall and with regard to the feeds of Hillary Clinton and Donald Trump.

This is not to say that bottom-up conceptualizations of the Twitter-to-news-media relationship do not exist. Research shows these relationships are often reciprocal and that social media are used to push unique campaign agendas (Conway et al. 2018), which news media are then likely to adopt (Kenski and Jamieson 2017; Metzgar and Maruggi 2009; Sayre et al. 2010). Agenda-building research also suggests "the media's impact on candidates' and parties' agendas is limited or even absent" during the campaign season (Walgrave and Van Aelst 2006: 96). As journalists increasingly use Twitter as a source for content, bottom-up relationships are increasingly likely. President Trump tweeted more than any politician in history, with an average of approximately 35 tweets per day during the final 6 months of his presidency (Way Back Machine 2021). Further, research suggests that news media, including *The New York Times* and *The Washington Post*, "give Trump front page coverage due to his power of attraction evinced in the tweets that his followers retweet the most" (Pérez-Curiel and Naharro 2019: 645).

No doubt, there were contextual factors in 2019–2020 that potentially exacerbated Trump's hold on newspapers, from his second impeachment trial to the global pandemic. Still, we followed the lead of previous studies on the presidential nomination season and predicted the following:

H1: During the 2020 presidential nomination season, reciprocal relationships existed between the issue agendas of newspapers and the issue agendas of candidate and campaign Twitter feeds.

H2: During the 2020 presidential nomination season, the issue agendas of newspapers predicted the issue agendas of candidate and campaign Twitter feeds to a greater extent than the reverse.

In addition to these hypotheses, we also examined Trump's and the Democratic frontrunner, Joe Biden's, ability to predict the newspaper agenda, allowing us to speak to the power of Trump and his main opposition. Here, we asked the following:

RQ1: During the 2020 presidential nomination season, did the Twitter feeds of the U.S. presidential election frontrunners predict the issue agendas of newspaper to a greater extent than the reverse?

Method

We replicated previous studies of the presidential nomination season (Conway, Kenski, and Wang 2015; Conway et al. 2018), using computer-assisted content analysis (CCA) to examine the issues that were emphasized by five of the nation's top newspapers and all viable presidential candidates and their parties during the 2020 presidential nomination season and time-series analysis to determine the relationship between the agendas of newspapers and those of Twitter feeds. While the overall analysis is based on separate newspaper and Twitter indices, with the latter combining the feeds of all presidential candidates and their campaigns, we also analyzed the two frontrunners, Biden and Trump. We then employed time-series analysis to examine the strength and direction of these relationships.

Data

We examined issue emphasis by five newspapers: *The Wall Street Journal, The New York Times, USA Today, The Los Angeles Times,* and *The Washington Post.* This selection aligned with previous studies' inclusion of the top-four newspapers in the nation (Pew 2019), as well as the inclusion of the largest newspaper on the West Coast. We collected articles published between January 1, 2020 and June 6, 2020 using Nexis Uni and ProQuest, including both online and print news stories. January 1 was the date used in previous studies due to its proximity to the Iowa caucuses, and June 6 was the day that Biden clinched the number of delegates needed to win the nomination of the Democratic Party. We retrieved articles using the search term "president*" in combination with "Republican Primar*," "Republican Caucus*," "Republican nomination," "Democratic Primar*," "Democratic Caucus*," "Democratic nomination," or any of the names of the candidates. All news articles and editorials that mentioned any of the candidates were included. If any of the returned articles did not reference one of the nominees or were deemed irrelevant, they were discarded, resulting in a total of 9,169 relevant articles, of which *The New York Times* had 4,524, *The Wall Street Journal* had 866, *USA Today* had 584, *The Los Angeles Times* had 839, and *The Washington Post* had 2,356.

The Twitter feeds of all major party candidates up until the date they dropped out of the race were included. They were first combined into a Twitter index ($N = 32,208$), which we used to test H1 and H2. Both certified individual candidate feeds and the certified feeds of their campaigns were collected using Twitter's REST application programming interface (API). If a candidate had a feed linked to their candidacy as well as a feed linked to their current political position (e.g., senator), both were included.[1] These data were exported into Excel files with several variables, including username, date of tweet, and tweet content. The totals for each Twitter feed can be found in Table 1.

Table 1. Twitter feeds included in overall Twitter index.

Twitter Handle	Total Tweets
Republicans	
@Mike_Pence	2,491
@VP	3,200
@RealDonaldTrump	4,633
@GovBillWeld	262
Total	10,586
Democrats	
@MichaelBennet	698
@TeamJoe	2,692
@JBiden	1,433
@MikeBloomberg	814
@Mike2020	1,582
@CoryBooker	57
@SenBooker	15
@PeteButtigieg	1,089
@PeteForAmerica	3,173
@JulianCastro	11
@JohnDelaney	189
@TulsiGabbard	426
@TulsiPress	48
@amyklobuchar	665
@SenAmyKlobuchar	23
@DevalPatrick	440
@TomSteyer	713
@TeamSteyer	1,361
@BernieSanders	1,529
@SenSanders	459
@ewarren	1,604
@TeamWarren	2,284
@SenWarren	317
@MichaelBennet	698
Total	21,622

Coding

We used QDA Miner to conduct the CCA and its supplementary program WordStat to produce issue tallies for the newspaper index and Twitter index/feeds. The unit of analysis for newspapers was all news articles published in the aforementioned newspapers that mentioned any of the presidential candidates or the presidential nomination contests on the days in question. The unit of analysis for Twitter data was all tweets posted by the included Twitter accounts on the days in question.

We started with the list of issues used in previous studies, as well as our dictionary, which has been developed over the past ten years (Conway, Kenski, and Wang 2015; Conway et al. 2018). We began by first dropping those issues that were no longer applicable (e.g., Zika, Benghazi, etc.). After applying valid categories from the previous dictionary to the Twitter and newspaper corpus and implementing any needed changes, Wordstat's "excluded words" option was used to examine thousands of words that appeared in the included articles and Twitter posts but were left out of the dictionary. Through this process, previous categories were further developed, and new categories were added, including one devoted to the COVID-19 pandemic. This resulted in a total of 28 categories.[2] Words, including hashtags, were only added to the dictionary if they appeared 10 or more times across the news articles and Twitter feeds.

Analysis

We first identified the top-five issues that appeared in the newspaper and Twitter indices, as well as the Twitter feeds of Trump and Biden. This resulted in 6 issues included in the analysis of H1 and H2 and the analysis of frontrunner agenda-setting power. The totals for all issues included in this analysis can be found in Table 2. While the content analysis was automated, follow-up validity checks were used to ensure the data were coded properly (Dang-Xuan et al. 2013).[3] Prior to examining relationships among our chosen sources, we first inspected each source for trends (both linear and quadratic) in order to remove patterns across our time-series data. The data for the two indices and those of Biden and Trump were then detrended to alleviate concerns of autocorrelation (Romer 2006). Cross-lagged correlations were then used to determine the strength of relationships between Twitter feeds and newspaper articles, offering insight into the predictive quality of each. In order to determine the power of these sources, two metrics were used. First, we examined the number of lags and leads, which indicate the number of days from one to seven (an entire week) that a given source was able to predict the other. Second, we examine the total number of issues (with a maximum of 6) that a given source was able to predict. Similar to previous studies, our results do not equate to causality (Sayre et al. 2010). Granger causality tests do indicate whether coefficients of past values in a regression model do not equate to zero—whether one variable (e.g., media issue emphasis) comes

Table 2. Total case occurrences by issue between Jan. 1 and June 6, 2020.

Issue		Newspaper Index	Twitter Index	Joe Biden	Donald Trump
COVID-19	Total (%)	68,910 (22.52)	2,251 (14.56)	198 (25.88)	814 (18.76)
	Rank	5	1	1	1
Economy	Total (%)	18,580 (6.55)	922 (5.96)	52 (6.80)	251 (5.78)
	Rank	2	5	4	5
Employment	Total (%)	14,165 (4.99)	1,224 (7.91)	72 (9.41)	297 (6.84)
	Rank	4	3	3	4
Foreign policy	Total (%)	43,947 (15.48)	1,459 (9.43)	42 (5.49)	642 (14.79)
	Rank	1	2	5	2
Government corruption	Total (%)	17,104 (6.03)	755 (4.88)	9 (1.18)	443 (10.21)
	Rank	12	8	19	3
Healthcare	Total (%)	19,584 (6.90)	1,201 (7.77)	83 (10.85)	162 (3.73)
	Rank	3	4	2	11

Note: Frequencies represent total mentions, while ranks and percentages represent case occurrence.

before another (e.g., Twitter issue emphasis) in the time series—with consistent patterns suggesting nonrandom associations.

Results

After creating the newspaper and Twitter indices for each issue examined, as well as separate data columns for Biden and Trump, curve estimation was used to detect linear and quadratic trends within daily frequencies for each of the four sources (i.e., Newspaper index, Twitter index, Trump, Biden) across the six issues included. These trends were then removed in order to test our hypotheses.

Before discussing the results of H1 and H2, it is important to note the convergence in issue ranking across the four sources. In previous analyses, choosing the top five sources resulted in 8 plus issues per analysis. In 2020, issue convergence was highly prevalent, likely due to the pandemic, resulting in most sources focusing heavily on COVID-19, the economy, (un)employment, foreign policy, and healthcare. While government corruption (the sixth issue explored in this study) was not in the top 10 for three of the four sources, it ranked third for Donald Trump, as he tweeted regularly about the impeachment trial and Hunter Biden's involvement with Burisma Holdings.

To address H1 and H2, we first tested the relationship between the Twitter and newspaper indices. H1 hypothesized the presence of reciprocal relationships between the Twitter index and the newspaper index. Based on a "Lead 0" for 5 out of 6 issues, reciprocal relationships were the norm (see Table 3). Same day relationships—represented by a lead of zero—show that both sources predicted one another on the same day. This, combined with the fact that both newspapers and Twitter influenced one another on a number of issues based on leads (representing newspapers predicting Twitter) and lags (representing Twitter predicting newspapers), supports H1.

Moving to H2, which predicted the newspaper index would out predict the Twitter index, in evaluating the number of leads and lags—our first metric—for the two sources, we found a clear tie. While Twitter exhibited 15 lags (in which Twitter predicted newspaper coverage) ranging from one to seven days, newspapers exhibited 15 leads also ranging from one to seven days. Thus, if we compare the total number of lags and leads, we see similar predictive power, especially given that the strength of these relationships was also quite similar.

Beyond lags and leads, if we look at specific issues—our second metric—newspapers led on five: COVID-19, employment, foreign policy, government corruption, and healthcare. Twitter, on the other hand, predicted newspapers on 2 out of 6 issues (COVID-19 and government corruption). Thus, in some cases Twitter led newspapers on COVID-19 emphasis, and in some cases, it was the reverse. For the first time in this line of research, H2 received only partial support.

Moving on to the predictive power of frontrunners Trump and Biden (RQ1), we once again find mixed results with regard to the power of newspapers. Beginning with Trump, his feed exhibited five lags ranging from one to seven days, while newspapers exhibited six leads ranging from one to four days. While newspapers exhibited 3 leads over Biden's feed ranging from one to seven days, Biden's feed exhibited four lags ranging from one to seven days. Thus, based on leads (representing newspapers predicting Biden or Trump) and lags (representing Biden or Trump predicting newspapers), we see almost equal power residing with the two platforms. With respect to specific issues, we see relatively equal predictive power for Biden compared to newspapers. While Biden exhibited lags on two of the six issues (COVID-19 and government corruption), newspapers also led on two (COVID-19 and foreign policy). For Trump, we see newspapers (potentially) win out. Newspapers led on four issues (COVID-19, the economy, employment, and government corruption), while Trump led on two (COVID-19 and government corruption).

Overall, our conclusions regarding newspapers' agenda-setting power over Twitter and the feeds of the frontrunners suggest relatively equal predictive power across the two platforms. Thus, newspapers exhibited less of a hold on Twitter issue content than what was found in past

Table 3. Significant cross-correlations between the newspaper index, Twitter index, and frontrunners.

Issue	Twitter Index	Joe Biden	Donald Trump
COVID-19	Lead 7: .24 Lead 6: .18 Lead 5: .19 Lead 4: .22 Lead 2: .23 Lead 1: .20 Lead 0: .28 Lag 1: .23 Lag 2: .15 Lag 3: .19 Lag 4: .16 Lag 5: .17 Lag 6: .23	Lead 7: .16 Lead 6: .18 Lead 0: .17 Lag 4: .18 Lag 7: .15	Lead 2: .15
Economy	None	None	Lead 4: .17
Employment	Lead 6: −.16 Lead 5: −.15 Lead 2: .15 Lead 0: .16	None	Lead 6: −.21 Lead 2: .19
Foreign policy	Lead 0: .15	Lead 1: .19 Lag 2: −.19	None
Government corruption	Lead 7: .17 Lead 6: .15 Lead 2: .24 Lead 1: .23 Lead 0: .24 Lag 1: .24 Lag 2: .17 Lag 3: .17 Lag 4: .15 Lag 5: .30 Lag 6: .26 Lag 7: .32	Lag 3: .16 Lag 1: .21	Lead 4: .17 Lead 2: .24 Lead 1: .17 Lag 1: .19 Lag 3: .24 Lag 4: .14 Lag 5: .31 Lag 7: .22
Healthcare	Lead 3: −.18 Lead 0: .19 Lag 3: −.16 Lag 4: −.21	Lead 4: −.17 Lead 3: −.17	Lead 3: −.18 Lag 2: −.20 Lag 4: −.15 Lag 5: −.18

Note: All cross-lagged correlations shown here are significant, $p < 0.05$. Leads shown indicate that newspapers predicted tweet emphasis a given number of days prior to the contemporary frequencies. Lags indicate that tweets predicted newspaper mentions a given number of days prior to the contemporary frequencies. Lag 0 indicates a contemporaneous relationship. Negative correlations indicate low incidence on Twitter.

research (Conway, Kenski, and Wang 2015; Conway et al. 2018). Furthermore, Trump exhibited the least predictive power across our four sources.

Discussion

Our goal was to discover whether relationships found in past intermedia agenda-setting studies of the Twitter-to-news-media relationship held during the 2020 presidential nomination season. Based on newspaper data, as well as Twitter data from all viable presidential candidates and their campaigns, computer-assisted content analysis (CCA) and time-series analysis were used to examine the strength and direction of these relationships. First, we find greater issue convergence in 2020 compared to previous elections, likely a result of contextual factors. Second, the relationships we uncover were once again reciprocal; however, they suggest greater similarity in predictive power between newspapers and Twitter than previous analyses. We are not willing to say that the scale has officially tipped toward Twitter—meaning Twitter predicted newspapers issue emphasis to a greater extent than the reverse—but we did find that the two platforms came closer to a level playing field with respect to their predictive power. Regardless of whether newspapers are listening, politicians on Twitter can carve their own metaphorical path and upend long-standing conceptualizations of the media's gatekeeping role (Bennett and Iyengar 2008). We explored the top-five issues here, but in future research we explore issue emphasis beyond the top-five, applying inter-candidate agenda setting and issue ownership.

In terms of the issues emphasized across our four sources, COVID-19 was highly prevalent (ranked first for all sources except newspapers, based on case occurrence), followed by the economy, healthcare, and major job loss, all of which are linked to the pandemic. Examining the dissimilarities, the Trump feed diverged from the Twitter index, newspaper index, and Biden feed in its emphasis on government corruption. Government corruption focused to a certain extent on the "lies" and general "corruption" coming out of the White House, but the bulk revolved around the impeachment trial of President Trump, including whether the trial was fair and whether anyone would be called to testify. Other topics emphasized included Trump's potential ties to Russia and Hunter Biden's ties to Burisma Holdings.

While some may argue for a separate category labeled "impeachment," governmental corruption is said to occur when those in power are involved in dishonest or fraudulent conduct associated in some way with their conduct in office. To hold the president, vice president, and civil officers accountable to their roles and responsibilities in the government, Article II, Section 4 of the U.S. Constitution states that, "The President, Vice President and all civil Officers of the United States, shall be removed from Office on Impeachment for, and Conviction of, Treason, Bribery, or other high Crimes and Misdemeanors." Presidential impeachment is a rare event having only happened four times in U.S. history. In the two cases carried out against Trump (abuse of power and obstruction of justice), they constitute examples of the president allegedly acting in a way that was corrupt because the acts involved misusing his presidential power, falling under the category of governmental corruption. The validity of separating impeachment from government corruption is questionable, though research would benefit from greater focus on the specific topic of impeachment.

Overall, it seems that newspapers as well as the Twitter sources, regardless of party affiliation, were responding to timely issues. The largest crosslagged correlations occurred for a lead of zero, implying that newspapers and Twitter sources were simultaneously responding to these issues. This differs from previous work suggesting that newspapers tend to lead Twitter with "ongoing discussions during non-breaking news periods" (Su and Borah 2019).

Given that Trump posted more tweets than any other Twitter feed included in this study yet saw the fewest significant relationships suggests that newspapers and the President diverged in their issue emphasis. In other words, his Twitter "power" did not apply to issue emphasis when it came to intermedia agenda setting among newspapers. Once again, the effects found by Wells and colleagues (2016) were not apparent when it came to important issues of the day. In the past, Trump was criticized for a lack of issue emphasis/knowledge (Kopan 2016). It is also possible that politicians who stray too far from the news media narrative or accuse them of wrongdoing, represented in his "fake news" accusations, might assume little traction. Further, it is quite possible that the newspapers included here were unwilling to peddle/engage with the misinformation and disinformation circulated by the Trump administration (Politifact 2021; Qui 2020). Thus, along with focusing on the issues and/or negativity, which are known to garner media attention, politicians would do well to focus on factual information. It is also possible that Trump's influence manifested in non-issue-related content. Along with investigating this, more research is needed beyond the "what," revealing "how" news media covered candidate tweets.

Whether these findings apply to news media beyond newspapers is an important question in need of further research. This study did not examine purely online news sources, cable news, or right-wing news sources. Fox, for example, has been accused of operating as a spokesperson for the Republican Party (Yglesias 2018). Examining intermedia agenda-setting relationships beyond the newspapers included here is warranted. We also used ProQuest and Lexis Uni to collect newspaper data. While this remains the most efficient way to gather such data, whether that truly reflects the 24-hour nature of newspaper functioning today is questionable. Others may criticize the examination of newspapers due to their slower publication cycle; however, research suggests even with a slower publication cycle, newspapers precede other media platforms, including websites and Twitter (Harder, Sevenans, and Van Aelst 2017). Further, due to them being held in high regard, newspaper coverage likely plays a legitimizing role for newer media.

Long-standing arguments that politicians and campaigns can use their funding and energy to set the media agenda (Dalton et al. 1998), including on social media (Neuman et al. 2014, Sayre et al. 2010), seem to win out. Unlike previous studies, Twitter and newspapers showed similar predictive power, suggesting that, even with a slower publication cycle, newspapers are still successful at predicting faster media forms. We argue this while recognizing the limitations of the current study. Given the number of influences outside of this study that are interacting with the two sources studied here, causation is not something we can determine. These not only include other media sources and campaign materials, but also members of the public and the social movements for which they are fighting. At the same time, given the growing body of research suggesting that journalists do tap Twitter for news content (Bane 2019; Hermida 2012; Lawrence 2015; Lecheler and Kruikemeier 2016), it is highly possible that these nonrandom relationships are demonstrating a level of Twitter-to-news-media influence. More research is needed to break down these relationships and understanding of Twitter's role in the election ecosystem for candidates, parties, and news media practitioners. Indeed, great work is currently being done to determine just how politicians go about engaging companies like Facebook and Twitter (Kreiss and McGregor 2018).

We also recognize the limitations of "issue" based intermedia agenda-setting analyses. Different ways of coding, from dictionary work to latent dirichlet processes (Guo et al. 2016) to the "news story" approach (Harder et al. 2017), have revealed different levels of accuracy. We are comforted by the decade long development of our dictionary, as well as the conservative nature of its application, while also recognizing its limits. By incorporating various media forms, coding processes, and engaging both quantitatively and qualitatively with media candidates, campaigns, and platforms, we are building a more complete picture of these agenda-setting influences—including those of the public.

Notes

1. @POTUS was not included because no original tweets were posted on this account during the time period specified.
2. Issues included energy, the environment, the First Amendment, foreign policy/relations, gender equality, government corruption, gun control/rights, healthcare, immigration, media credibility, military/veteran affairs, national security/terrorism/extremism, race/ethnic relations, social welfare, Supreme Court, taxes, and the war on drugs. Some of these issues are explored in other manuscripts.
3. Prior to analysis, a validity check was performed to ensure the data were coded properly with 60 references included for each source (Twitter vs. newspapers), 10 for each issue included. For Twitter, 94% of references were found to be valid, with individual issue agreement ranging from 80% to 100%. For newspapers, 91% of references were found to be valid, with individual issue agreement ranging from 80% to 100%.

References

Bane, K. C. 2019. "Tweeting the Agenda: How Print and Alternative Web-Only News Organizations Use Twitter as a Source." *Journalism Practice* 13 (2): 191–205. doi: 10.1080/17512786.2017.1413587.

Bendle, N. T. 2014. "Reference Dependence and Political Primaries." *Journal of Political Marketing* 13 (4): 307–33. doi: 10.1080/15377857.2012.721738.

Bennett, W. L, and S. Iyengar. 2008. "A New Era of Minimal Effects? The Changing Foundations of Political Communication." *Journal of Communication* 58 (4): 707–31. doi: 10.1111/j.1460-2466.2008.00410.x.

Bimber, B. 2014. "Digital Media in the Obama Campaigns of 2008 and 2012: Adaptation to the Personalized Political Communication Environment." *Journal of Information Technology & Politics* 11 (2): 130–50. doi: 10.1080/19331681.2014.895691.

Boyle, T. P. 2001. "Intermedia Agenda Setting in the 1996 Presidential Election." *Journalism & Mass Communication Quarterly* 78 (1): 26–44. doi: 10.1177/107769900107800103.

Ceron, A., L. Curini, and S. M. Iacus. 2016. "First- and Second-Level Agenda Building in the Twittersphere: An Application to the Italian Political Debate." *Journal of Information Technology & Politics* 13 (2): 159–74. doi: 10.1080/19331681.2016.1160266.

Conway, B. A., C. R. Filer, K. Kenski, and E. Tsetsi. 2018. "Reassessing Twitter's Agenda-Building Power: An Analysis of Intermedia Agenda-Setting Effects during the 2016 Presidential Primary Season." *Social Science Computer Review* 36 (4): 469–83. doi: 10.1177/0894439317715430.

Conway, B. A., K. Kenski, and D. Wang. 2015. "The Rise of Twitter in the Political Campaign: Searching for Intermedia Agenda-Setting Effects in the Presidential Primary." *Journal of Computer-Mediated Communication* 20 (4): 363–80. doi: 10.1111/jcc4.12124.

Clayton, J., L. Kelion, and D. Molloy. 2021. Trump allowed back onto Twitter. *BBC*. Retrieved from https://www.bbc.com/news/technology-55569604

Dalton, R. J., P. A. Beck, R. Huckfeldt, and W. Koetzle. 1998. "A test of mediacentered agenda setting: Newspaper content and public interests in a presidential election." *Political Communication* 15 (4): 463–481. doi: 10.1080/105846098198849.

Dang-Xuan, L., S. Stieglitz, J. Wladarsch, and C. Neuberger. 2013. "An Investigation of Influentials and the Role of Sentiment in Political Communication on Twitter during Election Periods." *Information, Communication & Society* 16 (5): 795–825. doi: 10.1080/1369118X.2013.783608.

Denham, B. E. 2010. "Toward Conceptual Consistency in Studies of Agenda-Building Processes: A Scholarly Review." *Review of Communication* 10 (4): 306–23. doi: 10.1080/15358593.2010.502593.

Dunn, S. W. 2009. "Candidate and Media Agenda Setting in the 2005 Virginia Gubernatorial Election." *Journal of Communication* 59 (3): 635–52. doi: 10.1111/j.1460-2466.2009.01442.x.

Enli, G., and C. Simonsen. 2018. "Social Media Logic' Meets Professional Journalism Norms: Twitter Hashtags Usage by Journalists and Politicians." *Information, Communication, & Society* 21 (8): 1081–96. doi: 10.1080/1369118X.2017.1301515.

Farhi, P. 2009. "The Twitter Explosion." American Journalism Review. Retrieved from http://www.ajr.org/Article.asp?id.4756.

Groshek, J., and M. C. Groshek. 2013. "Agenda Trending: Reciprocity and the Predictive Capacity of Social Networking Sites in Intermedia Agenda Setting across Topics over Time." *Media and Communication* 1 (1): 15–27. doi: 10.17645/mac.v1i1.71.

Guo, L., C. J. Vargo, Z. Pan, W. Ding, and P. Ishwar. 2016. "Big Social Data Analytics in Journalism and Mass Communication: Comparing Dictionary-Based Text Analysis and Unsupervised Topic Modeling." *Journalism & Mass Communication Quarterly* 93 (2): 332–59. doi: 10.1177/1077699016639231.

Harder, R. A., J. Sevenans, and P. Van Aelst. 2017. "Intermedia Agenda Setting in the Social Media Age: How Traditional Players Dominate the New Agenda in Election Times." *The International Journal of Press/Politics* 22 (3): 275–93. doi: 10.1177/1940161217704969.

Jacobson, S. 2013. "Does Audience Participation on Facebook Influence the News Agenda? A Case Study of the Rachel Maddow Show." *Journal of Broadcasting & Electronic Media* 57 (3): 338–55. doi: 10.1080/08838151.2013.816706.

Jungherr, A. 2016. "Twitter Use in Election Campaigns: A Systematic Literature Review." *Journal of Information Technology & Politics* 13 (1): 72–91. doi: 10.1080/19331681.2015.1132401.

Kapko, M. 2016. Twitter's impact on 2016 presidential election is unmistakable. CIO. Retrieved from https://www.sherbornma.org/sites/g/files/vyhlif1201/f/uploads/twitters_impact.pdf

Kendall, K. E. 2016. "Presidential Primaries and General Election Campaigns: A Comparison." In W. L. Benoit (Ed.), *Praeger Handbook of Political Campaigning in the United States* (31–60). Santa Barbara, CA: ABC-CLIO, LLC.

Kenski, K., and B. A. Conway. 2016. "Social Media and Elections." In W. L. Benoit (Ed.), *Praeger Handbook of Political Campaigning in the United States* (191–208). Santa Barbara, CA: ABC-CLIO, LLC.

Kenski, K., and K. H. Jamieson. 2017. "Political Communication: Looking Ahead." In K. Kenski & K. H. Jamieson (Eds.), *The Oxford Handbook of Political Communication* (913–8). New York: Oxford University Press.

Kopan, T. 2016. McConnell: "Obvious" Trump doesn't know issues. CNN. Retrieved from http://www.cnn.com/2016/06/10/politics/mitch-mcconnell-donald-trump-issues/

Kreiss, D. 2016. "Seizing the Moment: The Presidential Campaigns' Use of Twitter during the 2012 Electoral Cycle." *New Media & Society* 18 (8): 1473–90. doi: 10.1177/1461444814562445.

Kreiss, D., and S. McGregor. 2018. "Technology Firms Shape Political Communication: The Work of Microsoft, Facebook, Twitter, and Google with Campaigns during the 2016 U.S. presidential Cycle." *Political Communication* 35 (2): 155–77. doi: 10.1080/10584609.2017.1364814.

Lancendorfer, K. M, and B. Lee. 2010. "Who Influences Whom? The Agenda-Building Relationship between Political Candidates and the Media in the 2002 Michigan Governor's Race." *Journal of Political Marketing* 9 (3): 186–206. Retrieved from doi: 10.1080/15377857.2010.497737.

Lawrence, R. G. 2015. "Campaign News in the Time of Twitter." In V. A. Farrar-Meyers & J. S. Vaughn (Eds.), *Controlling the Message: New Media in American Political Campaigns* (93–112). New York: NYU Press.

Lecheler, S, and S. Kruikemeier. 2016. "Re-Evaluating Journalistic Routines in a Digital Age: A Review of Research on the Use of Online Sources." *New Media & Society* 18 (1): 156–71. doi: 10.1177/1461444815600412.

Lopez-Escobar, E., J. P. Llamas, M. McCombs, and F. R. Lennon. 1998. "Two Levels of Agenda Setting among Advertising and News in the 1995 Spanish Elections." *Political Communication* 15 (2): 225–38. doi: 10.1080/10584609809342367.

McCombs, M. 2004. *Setting the Agenda: The Mass Media and Public Opinion*. Malden, MA: Blackwell.

McClusky, M., and M. Zennie. 2021. Facebook blocks President Trump's account "indefinitely" after he incited mob that stormed capitol. *Time*. Retrieved from https://time.com/5926992/trump-video-twitter-risk-of-violence/

Meraz, S. 2009. "Is There an Elite Hold? Traditional Media to Social Media Agenda Setting Influence in Blog Networks." *Journal of Computer-Mediated Communication* 14 (3): 682–707. doi: 10.1111/j.1083-6101.2009.01458.x.

Metzgar, E., and A. Maruggi. 2009. "Social Media and the 2008 U.S." *Presidential Election. Journal of New Communications Research* 4:141–65.

Neuman, W. R., L. Guggenheim, S. M. Jang, and S. Y. Bae. 2014. "The Dynamics of Public Attention: Agenda Setting Theory Meets Big Data." *Journal of Communication* 64 (2): 193–214. doi: 10.1111/jcom.12088.

Parmelee, J. H. 2013a. "The Agenda-Building Function of Political Tweets." *New Media & Society* 16 (3): 434–50. doi: 10.1177/1461444813487955.

Parmelee, J. H. 2013b. "Political Journalists and Twitter: Influences on Norms and Practices." *Journal of Media Practice* 14 (4): 291–305. doi: 10.1386/jmpr.14.4.291_1.

Pew 2019. Newspaper fact sheet. *Pew*. Retrieved from https://www.journalism.org/fact-sheet/newspapers/

Perez-Curiel, C., and P. L. Naharro. 2019. "Political Influencers. A Study of Donald Trump's Personal Brand on Twitter and Its Impact on the Media and Users." *Communication and Society* 32:57–75.

Politifact 2021. Latest false fact checks on Donald Trump. *Politifact*. Retrieved from https://www.politifact.com/factchecks/list/?speaker=donald-trump&ruling=false

Quealy, K. 2021. The complete list of Trump's Twitter insults (2015-2021). *New York Times*. Retrieved from https://www.nytimes.com/interactive/2021/01/19/upshot/trump-complete-insult-list.html#

Qui, L. 2020. Hey @jack, here are more questionable tweets from @realdonaldtrump. *New York Times*. Retrieved from https://www.nytimes.com/2020/06/03/us/politics/trump-twitter-fact-check.html

Roberts, M., and M. McCombs. 1994. "Agenda Setting and Political Advertising: Origins of the News Agenda." *Political Communication* 11 (3): 249–62. doi: 10.1080/10584609.1994.9963030.

Rogstad, I. 2016. "Is Twitter just rehashing? Intermedia agenda setting between Twitter and mainstream media." *Journal of Information Technology & Politics* 13: 142–158. doi: 10.1080/19331681.2016.1160263.

Romer, D. 2006. "Time Series Models." In D. Romer, K. Kenski, K. Winneg, C. Adasiewicz, & K.H. Jamieson (Eds.), *Capturing Campaign Dynamics 2000 & 2004* (165–243). Pennsylvania, PA: University of Pennsylvania Press.

Ryoo, J., and N. Bendle. 2017. "Understanding the Social Media Strategies of U.S. primary Candidates." *Journal of Political Marketing* 16 (3–4): 244–66. doi: 10.1080/15377857.2017.1338207.

Sayre, B., L. Bode, D. Shah, D. Wilcox, and C. Shah. 2010. "Agenda Setting in a Digital Age." *Policy & Internet* 2 (2): 7–32. doi: 10.2202/1944-2866.1040.

Shapiro, M. A, and L. Hemphill. 2017. "Politicians and the Policy Agenda: Does Use of Twitter by the U.S. Congress Direst *New York Times* Content?" *Policy & Internet* 9 (1): 109–32. doi: 10.1002/poi3.120.

Shmargad, Y., and L. Sanchez. 2022. "Social Media Influence and Electoral Competition." *Social Science Computer Review* 40 (1): 4–23. doi: 10.1177/0894439320906803.

Stromer-Galley, J. 2014. *Presidential Campaigning in the Internet Age*. New York: Oxford University Press.

Su, Y., and P. Borah. 2019. "Who is the Agenda Setter? Examining the Intermedia Agenda-Setting Effect between Twitter Users and Newspapers." *Journal of Information Technology & Politics* 16 (3): 236–49. doi: 10.1080/19331681.2019.1641451.

Sweetser, K. D., G. J. Golan, and W. Wanta. 2008. "Intermedia Agenda Setting in Television, Advertising, and Blogs during the 2004 Election." *Mass Communication and Society* 11 (2): 197–216. doi: 10.1080/15205430701590267.

Towner, T. L, and D. A. Dulio. 2012. "New Media and Political Marketing in the United States: 2012 and beyond." *Journal of Political Marketing* 11 (1–2): 95–119. doi: 10.1080/15377857.2012.642748.

Van Aelst, P., J. Strömbäck, T.l Aalberg, F. Esser, C. de Vreese, J. Matthes, D. Hopmann, S. Salgado, N. Hubé, A. Stępińska, et al. 2017. "Political Communication in a High Choice Media Environment: A Challenge for Democracy?" Annals of the International Communication Association 41 (1): 3–27. doi: 10.1080/23808985.2017.1288551.

Vargo, C. J., E. Basilaia, and D. L. Shaw. 2015. "Event versus Issue: Twitter Reflections of Major News—A Case Study." *Communication and Information Technologies Annual—Studies in Media and Communications* 9:215–39. doi: 10.1108/S2050-206020150000009009.

Way Back Machine 2021. "The Twitter Trump Archive." *Internet Archive*. Retrieved from https://web.archive.org/web/20210109031942/https://www.thetrumparchive.com/.

Walgrave, S., and P. Van Aelst. 2006. "The Contingency of the Mass Media's Political Agenda Setting Power: Toward a Preliminary Theory." *Journal of Communication* 56 (1): 88–109. doi: 10.1111/j.1460-2466.2006.00005.x.

Weaver, D. H., and J. Choi. 2014. "The Media Agenda: Who (or What) Sets It?" In K. Kenski & K. H. Jamieson (Eds.), *The Oxford Handbook of Political Communication*. New York: Oxford University Press.

Wells, C., V. S. Dhavan, J. C. Pevehouse, J. H. Yang, A. Pelled, F. Boehm, J. Lukito, S. Ghosh, and J. L. Schmidt. 2016. "How Trump Drove Coverage to the Nomination: Hybrid Media Campaigning." *Political Communication* 33 (4): 669–76. doi: 10.1080/10584609.2016.1224416.

Yglesias, M. 2018. "The Case for Fox News Studies." *Political Communication* 35: 681–683. doi: 10.1080/10584609.2018.1477532.

An Application of Psychological Reactance Theory to College Student Voter Registration and Mobilization

Tobias Reynolds-Tylus and Dan Schill

ABSTRACT

The purpose of this study was to test political engagement messages (voter registration and voter mobilization) effectiveness with younger adults using psychological reactance theory as a guiding framework. Two online survey experiments using a 2 (message frame: gain- vs. loss-frame) X 2 (social norm: positive vs. negative) factorial design found that in the context of voter registration, consistent with prior research, both a loss-framed message and a positive norm message elicited greater freedom threat and reactance. However, these findings were not replicated in the context of voter mobilization. Across both topics, the arousal of reactance was associated with diminished behavioral intention (either for registering to vote or for voting). While the social norms approach has been found effective in mobilization campaigns, findings from this study demonstrate that an implicit threat to one's freedom (in the form of a positive social norms message) can elicit reactance among non-registered voters. This research suggests that political marketers should be aware of the potential for reactance to messages promoting voter registration among non-registered voters and be aware of potential backlash effects of loss-framed and positive norm-based messages in voter registration communication.

In most jurisdictions in the United States, voting is a two-step process. While 21 states and the District of Columbia allow registration on Election Day (as of 2020), most states require voters to register in advance—a process complicated by different procedures and deadlines in each state. Past research has found that voter registration rules are frequently a hurdle to voting and have historically been used to disenfranchise minority voters (for a review, see Mann and Bryant 2020). Requiring registration before Election Day is a major obstacle to participation and is associated with decreased registration and voting (Burden et al. 2014; Neiheisel and Burden 2012). Civic and political organizations promoting voting must encourage registering to vote prior to mobilizing citizens to go to the ballot box.

Voter mobilization campaigns have been widely studied and this research has dramatically changed how campaigns engage with voters to get out the vote (for a review, see Green and Gerber 2019). In contrast, voter registration communication is greatly understudied and the inconsistent findings in the existing research suggest the need for greater work in this area (Bennion and Nickerson 2016; Bryant et al. 2022; Mann and Bryant 2020). Focusing on this need, this study examines communication in both registration and mobilization campaigns.

Younger Americans have lower levels of political engagement (both voter registration and voting behavior) than other age cohorts. In 2016, for example, 17.4% of registrants were between the ages of 18 and 29, 22.9% were aged 30 to 44, 36.4% were aged 45 to 64, and 23.3% were

65 and older (File 2018). In terms of voting, the disparity was even greater in 2016, with Americans between 18 and 29 making up 15.7% of voters (File 2018). These trends are not new. Younger people (age 18 to 29) have consistently voted at lower rates than all other age groups since the U.S. Census Bureau began tracking voter turnout (File 2014). As a group, younger voters face several hurdles to participation: they are highly mobile and more difficult to contact and engage, they are less likely to have strong ties to political parties, they may not have a habit of participation, and they are more likely to be first-time voters, among other impediments (Bennion and Nickerson 2019). Nonprofit organizations, including college campuses, frequently initiate campaigns to boost registration and turnout, however, much of these efforts rely on past practice and anecdotal evidence when designing their outreach activities. The purpose of this study is to test the effectiveness of political engagement messages (voter registration and voter mobilization) with younger adults using psychological reactance theory (Brehm 1966; Brehm and Brehm 1981) as a guiding framework.

Psychological reactance theory

Psychological reactance theory provides an explanation for how individuals react when a valued personal freedom is eliminated or threatened (Brehm 1966; Brehm and Brehm 1981). Psychological reactance theory is based on the premise that individuals cherish their ability to make decisions autonomously. Anything that makes a particular freedom more difficult to enact constitutes a freedom threat. Persuasive messages by their very nature can be freedom-threatening, as they either implicitly or explicitly encourage individuals to perform (or avoid) a particular behavior.

Psychological reactance is "the motivational state that is hypothesized to occur when a freedom is eliminated or threatened with elimination" (Brehm and Brehm 1981, 37). Reactance has been shown to be comprised of both anger and negative thoughts (Dillard and Shen 2005; Rains 2013), preceded by a perceived freedom threat (Quick and Stephenson 2008). Individuals who experience reactance are motivated to restore their freedom either directly (e.g., directly engaging in the restricted behavior) or indirectly (e.g., discounting the credibility of the message or the messenger; Brehm 1966; Brehm and Brehm 1981). In political contexts, scholars have observed that strong social pressure messages to vote may be perceived as heavy handed and backfire on the communicator by prompting reactance (Gerber, Green, and Larimer 2008; Mann 2010; Matland and Murray 2013). Research has shown that the unintentional arousal of reactance is associated with a variety of undesirable persuasive outcomes, including diminished attitudes and behavioral intentions, as well as lower source and message evaluations (see Quick, Shen, and Dillard 2013; Reynolds-Tylus 2019).

While the majority of research indicates reactance arousal is associated with negative outcomes, a study from Daniel Biggers (2021) hypothesized that intentionally eliciting reactance may encourage turnout. Specifically, Biggers (2021) assessed if a message to minority voters emphasizing voter suppression might motivate turn out by activating the desire to overcome such restrictions. Biggers found that while a psychological reactance framing of voter ID laws as an attack on their right to vote did trigger reactance from African American voters by reducing their support of the policy and increasing the law's perceived threat to their franchise, such framing did not ultimately influence their voting behavior in field experiments. That is, while reactance was elicited to change attitudes, it did not significantly change behaviors.

Considering the unintentional elicitation of reactance can have undesirable consequences, researchers have examined strategies for circumventing or diminishing reactance among target audiences (Quick, Shen, and Dillard 2013; Reynolds-Tylus 2019). For instance, studies have consistently found that messages which are explicit, vivid, and use concrete language with a clear intent to persuade are likely to elicit greater reactance than messages that are implicit, choice-enhancing, and autonomy-supporting (see Mann 2010; Reynolds-Tylus 2019; Rosenberg and Siegel 2018). The current investigation examines two message features—message frame (gain vs. loss) and norm (positive vs. negative)—and their association with psychological reactance in the context of voter registration and mobilization.

Message framing

A large body of literature has compared the persuasiveness of gain- vs. loss-framed messages (Nan, Daily, and Qin 2018; O'Keefe 2012; O'Keefe and Jensen 2006, 2007, 2009). Gain-framed messages focus on the benefits of adopting a recommended action (e.g., voting is a way ensure your views are represented at the local, state, and federal level) whereas loss-framed messages focus on the costs of failing to adopt the recommended action (e.g., by not voting, your views are not being represented at the local, state, and federal level). Loss-framed messages are theorized to be more persuasive than gain-framed messages due to two psychological phenomena—negativity bias and loss aversion (O'Keefe 2012). Negativity bias refers to the heightened impact of, and sensitivity to, negative information (Cacioppo, Gardner, and Berntson 1997). Negative events and stimuli evoke stronger and more rapid responses than positive ones (Taylor 1991). Loss-aversion refers to a conceptually similar phenomena, whereby individuals show a preference for avoiding losses when compared to obtaining gains (Kahneman, Knetsch, and Thaler 1990; Kahneman and Tversky 1979). Due to both negativity bias and loss aversion, loss-framed messages have been theorized to be more persuasive than gain-framed messages (O'Keefe 2012). Meta-analyses by O'Keefe and Jensen (2006, 2007, 2009), however, have failed to find support for a persuasive advantage of one frame over another.

Registration and voter mobilization campaigns frequently use gain-framed messages (e.g., benefits, aspirations) and loss-framed messages (e.g., threat, harm). While laboratory experiments often find loss-frames produce larger effects, other research, especially field experiments often find mixed or contradictory results (Mann, Arceneaux, and Nickerson 2020). Panagopoulos (2010), for example, found that on average messages accentuating a negative frame ("shame") were more effective at engendering political participation than messages underscoring a positive frame ("pride"), but the distinction depended on the type of recipient with shame motivating compliance amongst low- and high-propensity voters and pride only mobilizing high-propensity voters (see also, Gerber, Green, and Larimer 2010). On the other hand, in a large-scale field experiment, Miller and Krosnick (2004) found that people were more likely to participate in political activism if a change from the status quo was framed as an opportunity rather than a threat.

Psychological reactance has been proposed as an explanation for differences in the effectiveness of gain- vs. loss-framed messages. Compared to gain-framed messages, loss-framed messages have been theorized to be more freedom threatening, and accordingly arouse greater reactance (Nan, Daily, and Qin 2018; O'Keefe 2012). Therefore, the arousal of reactance should offset the persuasive advantages of loss-framed messages—negativity bias and loss aversion (O'Keefe 2012; Shen 2015). Several researchers have tested the hypothesis that loss-framed messages arouse greater freedom threat and reactance than gain-framed messages (Reinhart et al. 2007; Quick and Bates 2010; Cho and Sands 2011; Quick et al. 2015; Shen 2015). The evidence, however, has been mixed. Some studies have found that loss-framed messages elicit greater freedom threat and reactance than gain-framed messages, thus undermining the persuasive advantage of loss-framed messages (Reinhart et al. 2007; Shen 2015; Zhao and Nan 2010). Other studies have found either no support (Quick and Bates 2010; Quick et al. 2015) or inconsistent support (Cho and Sands 2011; Lee and Cameron 2017) for this proposition. Accordingly, the current study seeks to test the proposition that a loss-frame message will elicit greater freedom threat and subsequent reactance than a gain-framed message. Therefore, the following hypotheses are proposed:

H1: A loss-frame message will elicit greater freedom threat than a gain-frame message.

H2: Freedom threat will be positively associated with reactance.

Reactance is a motivational state that directs behavior (Brehm 1966; Brehm and Brehm 1981). The unintentional arousal of reactance has been associated with a variety of negative persuasive outcomes, including diminished behavioral intentions (Quick, Shen, and Dillard 2013; Reynolds-Tylus 2019). Therefore, the following hypothesis is proposed:

H3: Reactance will be negatively associated with intention to [register to vote/vote].

Social norms

Social norms are defined as socially negotiated and enforced codes of conduct that prescribe or proscribe behavior for members of a particular group (Cialdini, Reno, and Kallgren 1990; Lapinski and Rimal 2005). The impact of social norms on human behavior has been long documented (Asch 1951; Sherif 1936). Given the influence of social norms on individual's behavior (Chung and Rimal 2016), a common communication strategy for promoting behavior is to modify perceptions of social norms among a target audience in order to encourage action (Perkins and Berkowitz 1986). Norms-based messaging has been applied widely in political, health, and environmental contexts (Green and Gerber 2019; Miller and Prentice 2016). However, evidence on the overall effectiveness of social norms messaging has been mixed (Campo et al. 2003; Miller and Prentice 2016).

The social norms approach has been extensively studied in political marketing contexts. These studies typically examine direct mail messages that show subjects their own as well as their neighbors' prior voting history (e.g., Panagopoulos, Larimer, and Condon 2014). In their meta-analysis, Green, McGrath, and Aronow (2013) concluded that when asserted forcefully, social pressure messages significantly increase turnout, but that subtle framings sometime fail to produce large effects. Similarly, based on field experimental evidence from 1.96 million citizens in 17 States, Gerber et al. (2017, 555) determined that "activating social norms about voting is a consistently effective means for increasing turnout." For example, Haenschen and Jennings (2019) found that ads emphasizing high turnout intended to create a descriptive social norm of participation increased turnout among Millennial voters in competitive races when combined with an ad promoting a local newspaper's coverage of local races.

Extensive research has attempted to determine if positive social norms (e.g., "many people vote") or negative social norms (e.g., "few people vote") are more or less impactful on voting behavior. Research on positively framed vs. negatively framed social norms is mixed. Some existing research finds that people are more likely to say they will vote when they hear lots of people are voting than when they hear a message lamenting low voter turnout (Gerber and Rogers 2009; Murray and Matland 2014), while other research identified no effect of positive social descriptive norms on verified voter turnout (Bhatti et al. 2017; Gerber et al. 2018; Keane and Nickerson 2015; Panagopoulos, Larimer, and Condon 2014). Other research finds that negatively framed messages are most impactful on political behavior, especially when they generate anger in individuals (Hassell and Wyler 2019). Negative social norms messages may decrease turnout. Keane and Nickerson's (2015) study of young Latino voters in Colorado during the 2008 presidential election found that a message emphasizing negative social norms—that only 20% of young Latinos actually voted in 2006—was associated with a decrease in turnout by 1.2 percentage points compared to a control group. In the same study, a positive social norm message—the 90% of Latinos planned to participate in the historic election—had no effect on voters in this cohort. These results are echoed in a field study in Denmark, where Bhatti et al. (2017) found that positive social norm text messages ("Your friends are voting at the election tomorrow. They are counting on you to do the same. Don't fail them. VOTE!") had no significant effect on voting compared to informational message framings.

Gerber et al. (2018, 1000) identify "the need for future research investigating the conditions under which framing descriptive norms about voting either positively or negatively in a mobilization campaign have distinguishable effects on turnout and, more generally, how individuals psychologically and behaviorally respond to specific normative appeals when they are bundled with other normative and informational appeals (as is likely in real-world interventions)." This study attempts to address this need by examining the interplay among social norms (positive vs. negative) and psychological reactance in the context of voter registration and mobilization.

Psychological reactance theory proposes that any persuasive message holds the potential to elicit reactance if the message recipient perceives their freedom to be threatened by the message (Brehm 1966; Brehm and Brehm 1981). Though reactance is more likely to occur in response to messages that are overly forceful, domineering, and explicitly persuasive (Quick, Shen, and Dillard 2013; Reynolds-Tylus 2019), reactance can also occur in response to more implied threats to one's freedom (Brehm 1966; Brehm and Brehm 1981). Positive social norm messages may implicitly threaten individuals' freedoms in several ways. For instance, a message emphasizing a positive descriptive norm (e.g., "many people vote") implicitly suggests that one *should* vote. Furthermore, social norms messages also suggest social sanctions for behavioral action or inaction (Cialdini, Reno, and Kallgren 1990; Lapinski and Rimal 2005). For instance, a positive descriptive norm message highlighting that many people vote may imply that if one does not vote, they will be viewed negatively by others. The current study seeks to examine this hypothesis in the context of voter registration and mobilization messages. Therefore, the following hypothesis is proposed:

H4: *A positive norm message will elicit greater freedom than a negative norm message.*

The current study

Below, we report on data from two studies, one on voting registration and one on voter mobilization. Data for voter registration study was conducted in the spring of 2020 with a sample of non-registered voters. Data for the voter mobilization study was conducted in fall of 2020 with a sample of participants who had not voted. Both studies were online survey experiments using a 2 (frame: gain- vs. loss-frame) X 2 (norm: positive vs. negative) factorial design. The procedures and analyses were identical for both studies, so the method and results for both samples are reported together.

Method

Participants and procedures

Participants were recruited from university-wide introductory public speaking classes at James Madison University[1] after receiving IRB approval. Participants were eligible to complete the survey if they were 18 years of age or older and U.S. citizens. For the voter registration study, an additional requirement was that participants were not currently registered to vote. For both studies, participants received a small amount of course credit for completing the survey.

For the voter registration study, an initial sample of 240 participants were recruited. Only those participants who passed two attention checks ($n = 151$) were retained for analysis. Participants ($n = 151$) ranged in age from 18 to 29 ($M = 18.65$, $SD = 1.01$). Most participants reported their gender as male (51.7%), followed by female (47.7%). One participant (0.7%) identified as a transgender female/transgender woman. Most participants reported their race/ethnicity[2] as White or Caucasian (85.4%), followed by Asian (9.3%), Hispanic, Latino, or Spanish origin (5.3%), African American or Black (4.0%), and American Indian or Alaskan Native (0.7%). Three participants (2.0%) identified as some other race. The majority of participants were first-year students (92.7%), followed by Sophomores (6.0%), and Juniors (1.3%).

For the voter mobilization study, an initial sample of 464 participants were recruited. Participants who failed either of two attention check items ($n = 114$) were removed from the final analysis. Participants ($n = 115$) who had already voted were also removed. Participants ($n = 235$) ranged in age from 18 to 26 ($M = 18.23$, $SD = 0.87$). Most participants reported their gender as female (79.1%), followed by male (18.9%). Most participants reported their race/ethnicity as White or Caucasian (88.1%), followed by Hispanic, Latino, or Spanish origin (5.5%), Asian (5.5%), African American or Black (5.1%), and American Indian or Alaskan Native (0.4%). The majority of participants were first-year students (93.2%), followed by Sophomores (2.6%), and Juniors (3.4%). The vast majority of participants (88.9%) were registered to vote.

In the voter registration study, most participants identified as Republican (53.6%), followed by independent (26.5%), and Democrat (18.5%). In the voter mobilization study, most participants identified as a Democrat (35.3%), followed by Republican (34.5%), and independent (29.8%). Participants had somewhat strong political affiliations for both studies (registration: $M=2.11$, $SD=1.11$; mobilization: $M=2.59$, $SD=1.20$; measured on a 5-point Likert scale: 1 = *not strong at all*, 2 = *somewhat strong*, 3 = *moderately strong*, 4 = *strong*, and 5 = *very strong*).

After providing informed consent, participants were randomly assigned to one of four experimental conditions in a 2 (frame: gain vs. loss) x 2 (norm: positive vs. negative) factorial[3] design. Participants were instructed to read the message carefully before moving on to the next page. Following message exposure, participants completed all study measures and a demographic questionnaire.

Message stimuli

The message stimuli (see Figure 1 for the messages from the registration study) were posters designed to resemble real-life voter registration and mobilization advertisements at James Madison University by using the university's color scheme and by using the nickname ("Dukes") for the student population. Messages ranged from 9 to 12 words in length (depending on the condition). The first line of the poster conveyed with the normative information. The negative norm message read, "Few Dukes vote." The positive norm message read, "Many Dukes vote." The second line conveyed the message frame. The gain-frame message read, "Make your voice heard this November." The loss-frame message read, "Don't be silenced this November." All messages concluded with a call to action, "Register to vote" (registration study) or "Vote" (mobilization study).

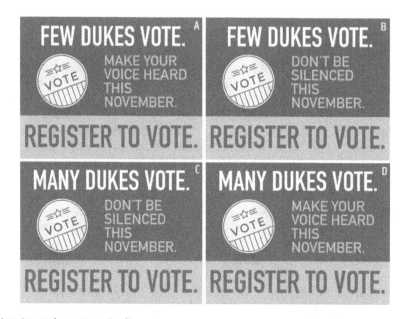

Figure 1. Registration study message stimuli.
Note. A = Negative Norm × Gain Frame, B = Negative Norm × Loss Frame, C = Positive Norm × Loss Frame, D = Positive Norm × Gain Frame.

Measures

For both studies, items were measured on a 5-point Likert scale (1 = *strongly disagree* to 5 = *strongly agree*). See Table 1 for a zero-order correlation matrix for all measured variables.

Reactance

Reactance is conceptualized as a two-step process consisting of a freedom threat followed by state reactance, measured as anger and negative cognitions (Dillard and Shen 2005; Quick and Stephenson 2008; Rains 2013). Freedom threat was measured with four items (e.g., "The message I just read threatened my freedom to choose," registration study: α = .89, M = 2.39, SD = 0.93; mobilization study: α = .85, M = 2.09, SD = 0.87) from Dillard and Shen (2005). Anger was measured with four items (e.g., "Reading the message made me feel angry," registration study: α = .94, M = 1.89, SD = 0.87; mobilization study: α = .95, M = 1.83, SD = 0.90) from Dillard and Shen (2005). Negative cognitions were measured with three items (e.g., "The thoughts I had while reading this message were mostly unfavorable," registration study: α = .91, M = 2.14, SD = 0.88; mobilization study: α = .93, M = 1.99, SD = 0.93) from Reynolds-Tylus, Bigsby, and Quick (2021).

Intention

Intention was measured with three items (e.g., "[Registering to vote/Voting] is something I plan to do soon," registration study: α = .97, M = 3.97, SD = 0.99; mobilization study: α = .98, M = 4.63, SD = 0.69) based on recommendations from Fishbein and Ajzen (2010).

Results

Preliminary analyses

Induction checks

The manipulation of message frame (gain vs. loss) and norm (positive vs. negative) were successful for both studies. Participants in the loss-frame (registration study: M = 3.12, SD = 1.08; mobilization study: M = 3.08, SD = 1.11) condition were more likely to agree with the statement "The message I read earlier focused on the costs of NOT voting" than those in the gain-frame (registration study: M = 2.39, SD = 0.98; mobilization study: M = 2.34, SD = 0.94) condition for both the registration study, $t(1, 149)$ = −1.93, p < .001, d = .71, and mobilization study, $t(1,$

Table 1. Zero-order correlation matrix for study variables.

Variable	1	2	3	4	5	6	7	8	9	10
1. Message frame (0 = loss, 1 = gain)	----	−.05	−.01	.04	.05	−.06	.03	.05	−.08	−.02
2. Norm message (0 = negative, 1 = positive)	.03	----	.02	−.22**	−.21**	.05	−.01	.04	−.03	.06
3. Freedom threat	−.19**	.18**	----	.46**	.48**	−.25**	−.13	.07	.06	−.13
4. Anger	−.02	.11	.52**	----	.77**	−.24**	−.15*	.05	.10	−.04
5. Negative cognitions	−.00	.11	.46**	.70**	----	−.26**	−.25**	.12	.14*	−.11
6. Intention	−.04	.18**	−.16	−.35**	−.35**	----	.16*	−.19**	.02	.41**
7. Democrat	−.02	−.08	−.13	−.07	−.10	.17*	----	−.48**	−.54**	.14*
8. Independent	.02	.12	.17*	.20*	.27**	−.23**	−.29**	----	−.48**	−.11
9. Republican	−.01	−.04	−.05	−.12	−.17*	.06	−.53**	−.66**	----	−.04
10. Registered to vote [mobilization study only]	----	----	----	----	----	----	----	----	----	----

Note.
*p < .05,
**p < .01. Correlations for the registration study are reported on the left of the diagonal. Correlations for the voter mobilization study are reported on the right of the diagonal. Democrat, independent, Republican, and Registered to Vote were all coded such that 0 = no, 1 = yes.

233) = 5.55, $p < .001$, $d = .72$. Likewise, participants in the positive norm (registration study: $M = 3.40$, $SD = 0.85$; mobilization study: $M = 4.01$, $SD = 0.65$) condition were more likely to agree with the statement "Most James Madison University students are [registered to vote/vote]" than those in the negative norm (registration study: $M = 3.03$, $SD = 0.95$; mobilization study: $M = 3.56$, $SD = 0.86$) condition for both registration study, $t(1, 149) = -2.55$, $p = .012$, $d = .41$, and mobilization study, $t(1, 233) = -4.51$, $p < .001$, $d = .59$.

Direct effects

In the registration study, participants who viewed the negative norm message ($M = 4.17$, $SD = 0.89$) had higher intention to register to vote than those who viewed the positive norm ($M = 3.81$, $SD = 1.04$) message, $t(1, 148) = 2.28$, $p = .024$, $d = .38$. Participants in the registration study did not differ in their intention to register to vote based on message frame, $t(1, 148) = 0.48$, $p = .631$, $d = .08$. For the mobilization study, participants did not differ in their intention to vote depending on message frame, $t(1, 233) = 0.87$, $p = .387$, $d = .12$, or norm, $t(1, 233) = -0.76$, $p = .450$, $d = 10$.

Data analytic procedures

Study hypotheses were examined using structural equation modeling[4] with maximum likelihood robust estimation in Mplus 8.0 for Mac. Model fit was considered "good" when CFI $\geq .95$ and SRMR $\leq .08$ (Kline 2016). Model fit was considered "acceptable" when CFI $\geq .90$ and SRMR $\leq .09$ (Holbert and Stephenson 2008). RMSEA was not reported as the sample size for both studies was < 250 (Holbert and Stephenson 2008). In line with recommendations from Kline (2016), a two-step analysis procedure was utilized. All latent factors underwent a confirmatory factor analysis prior to testing the structural model.

Confirmatory factor analysis

The hypothesized models for both studies contained five latent variables: (a) freedom threat, (b) anger, (c) negative cognitions, (d) reactance (modeled as a second-order latent factor comprised of anger and negative cognitions), and (e) intention. Message frame (0 = loss-frame, 1 = gain-frame) and norm message (0 = negative, 1 = positive) were modeled as observed variables and thus were not included in the measurement model. The measurement model demonstrated acceptable fit for both the registration study, $\chi^2(72, N = 142) = 163.28$, CFI $= .92$, SRMR $= .05$, and good fit for the mobilization study, $\chi^2(72, N = 235) = 120.59$, CFI $= .96$, SRMR $= .04$.

Main analysis

The structural model demonstrated acceptable fit for the registration study, $\chi^2(109, N = 140) = 233.53$, $p < .001$, CFI $= .91$, SRMR $= .06$, and good fit for the mobilization study, $\chi^2(138, N = 235) = 239.41$, $p < .001$, CFI $= .95$, SRMR $= .07$. The unstandardized (UPC) and standardized (SPC) path coefficients are presented in the next paragraph. See Figure 2 for a visual representation of the structural models. Given the relationships between covariates and study variables (see Table 1), one covariate (independent: 0 = no, 1 = yes) was included in the model for the registration study, and three covariates (Democrat, independent, and voter registration [all coded: 0 = no, 1 = yes]) were included in the model for the mobilization study.

H1 predicted a negative association between a gain-framed message and freedom threat. H1 was supported for the registration (UPC $= -.33$/SPC $= -.18$, $p = .033$) but not for the mobilization study (UPC $= -.09$/SPC $= -.06$, $p = .443$). H2 predicted a positive association between freedom threat and reactance. H2 was supported for both the registration study (UPC $= .49$/SPC $= .63$, $p < .001$) and the mobilization study (UPC $= .56$/SPC $= .62$, $p < .001$). H3 predicted a negative

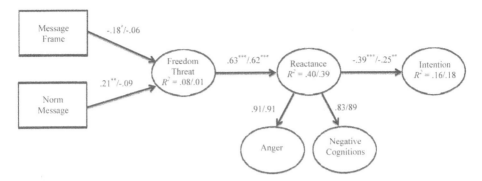

Figure 2. Structural models for voter registration study and mobilization study.
Note. Standardized estimates and R^2 are listed first for the registration study, $\chi^2(109, N=140) = 233.53$, $p < .001$, CFI = .91, SRMR = .06, followed by the mobilization study, $\chi^2(138, N=235) = 239.41$, $p < .001$, CFI = .95, SRMR = .07. Message frame was coded such that 0 = loss-frame, 1 = gain-frame. Norm message was coded such that 0 = negative norm, 1 = positive norm. Covariates are not shown in the model. *$p < .05$, **$p < .01$, ***$p < .001$.

association between reactance and intention (either to register to vote or to vote). H3 was supported for both the registration study (UPC = −.55/SPC = −.39, $p < .001$) and the mobilization study (UPC = −.17/SPC = −.25, $p = .002$). H4 predicted a positive association between a positive norm message and freedom threat. H4 was supported for the registration study (UPC = .38/SPC = .25, $p = .011$), but not for the mobilization study (UPC = −.14/SPC = −.09, $p = .225$).

For the registration study, the indirect effect of message frame (gain- vs. loss-) on reactance as mediated by freedom threat was significant (UPC = −.16/SPC = −.11, $p = .042$). The indirect effect of norm (positive vs. negative) on reactance as mediated by freedom threat was significant (UPC = .19/SPC = .13, $p = .023$). The indirect effect of freedom threat on intention as mediated by reactance was significant (UPC = −.27/SPC = −.25, $p = .012$). For the mobilization study, the indirect effect of freedom threat on intention as mediated by reactance was significant (UPC = −.09/SPC = −.16, $p = .005$). No other indirect effects were significant for either study. In all, the structural models accounted for the following variance in endogenous variables, for the registration study and the mobilization study, respectively: (a) freedom threat ($R^2 = .08, .01$), (b) reactance ($R^2 = .40, .39$), and (c) intention ($R^2 = .16, .18$).

Discussion

The current study used psychological reactance theory (Brehm 1966; Brehm and Brehm 1981) as a guiding framework for examining messages promoting political engagement (voter registration and mobilization) among a sample of college-aged students. We hypothesized that a loss-framed message would elicit greater freedom threat and reactance than a gain-framed message. Likewise, we hypothesized a positive norm message ("Many Dukes vote") would elicit greater freedom threat and reactance than a negative norm message ("Few Dukes vote"). In the context of voter registration, consistent with these expectations, both a loss-framed message and a positive norm message elicited greater freedom threat and reactance. However, these findings were not replicated in the context of voter mobilization. Across both topics, the arousal of reactance was associated with diminished behavioral intention (either for registering to vote or for voting).

Psychological reactance has been proposed as an explanation for the ineffectiveness of loss-framed messages (Nan, Daily, and Qin 2018; O'Keefe 2012). Consistent with this proposition, we found that in the context of voter registration, a loss-framed message elicited greater freedom threat and reactance than a gain-framed message. However, no differences between gain- vs. loss-framed messages in terms of freedom threat and reactance were observed in the context of voter mobilization. When considering whether to employ gain- or loss-framed messages in registration campaigns, political marketers would do well to anticipate and account for likely freedom threat reactions (see Mann, Arceneaux, and Nickerson 2020). In the current study, the benefits of voting were framed as being heard ("Make your voice heard this November") whereas the costs of not voting were framed as being silenced ("Don't be silenced this November"). Results from the current study suggest the ineffectiveness of this particular type of loss-frame messaging (being silenced) for promoting voter registration among those currently not registered to vote. Given that the benefits and costs of (not) voting can be framed in several ways, future research would benefit from alternative operationalizations of gain- vs. loss-framing in this context.

In line with previous research (Gerber, Green, and Larimer 2008; Matland and Murray 2013), the current study demonstrates that messages emphasizing positive normative support for voter registration may backfire (due to increased psychological reactance) among individuals who are currently not registered to vote. Reactance research has most commonly examined messages with explicit threats to one's freedom compared to non-threatening messages (see Rains 2013). While the social norms approach is effective in mobilization campaigns (Gerber et al. 2017; Haenschen and Jennings 2019), findings from the current study demonstrate that an implicit threat to one's freedom (in the form of a positive social norms message) can elicit reactance among non-registered voters. This finding should be contextualized somewhat given the campus environment in which data were collected. At James Madison University (where data were collected) approximately 80% of the student population was registered to vote. Notably, the current message strategy for the university's center for civic engagement relies heavily on normative messaging (e.g., "Dukes vote"). Results from the current study suggest this type of positive norms messaging has the potential to backfire, at least among those currently not registered to vote.

Notably, the present study used equivalent methods to test similar message elements among young adults in two contexts—registration and mobilization—and found differing results. This is an important reminder for political marketers that registration and mobilization are distinct persuasive situations that likely require different communicative strategies. Correspondingly, communication directed to moving a non-registrant to an active voter may be a two-step process. Understanding the differing attitudes and motivations between non-registered individuals and registered, late or nonvoters is outside the scope of this study; however, future research should continue to study persuasion in these two contexts and how registered and non-registered individuals may differ.

Limitations and future directions

The current study has several limitations worth mentioning. First, participants viewed the experimental messages with the knowledge they were participating in a research study and that their perceptions of the message were of chief interest. Second, the current study used a factorial design with no control condition—without a control message to compare our results to, we can't say whether or not any particular message 'backfired' (as we had no baseline to compare registration and voting intentions to). Third, the current study is also limited by the population sampled. Data were collected at a single university and participants were mostly White and female which may limit the generalizability of the study. Finally, the dependent variables studied were behavioral intention and not actual behavior. Future research would benefit from longitudinal designs and/or field studies that allow for the assessment of behavioral outcomes.

Conclusion

In summary, this study found that in a registration context, both a loss-framed message ("Don't be silenced") and a positive norm message ("Many college students vote") were associated with greater freedom threat. No differences in freedom threat were observed in the context of mobilization. In both contexts, when participants perceived a threat to their freedom, they experienced greater reactance and subsequently diminished intention (either to register to vote or to vote). Accordingly, political marketers should be aware of the potential for reactance to messages promoting voter registration among non-registered voters and be aware of potential backlash effects of loss-framed and positive norm-based messages in voter registration communication. Our results also serve as a reminder that voter registration and mobilization require different communication strategies. In both contexts, communicators would be well served to consider and forestall potential reactance. Future work should continue to examine the role of reactance in political marketing.

Notes

1. James Madison University is a public university located in Harrisonburg, Virginia. The student population is approximately 21,500 and is comprised of predominately full-time (90%) and undergraduate (90.5%) students from Virginia and surrounding states. James Madison University sponsors year-round voter education and engagement initiatives through curriculum and a civic engagement center.
2. Percentages may not add up to 100% as participants were able to select one or more categories for race/ethnicity.
3. We did not include a no-message control condition as the purpose of the study was to study reactance, which reflects individuals' reactions to a message stimulus.
4. Structural equation modeling was used for analyses as reactance is hypothesized to be multi-step process whereby freedom threat precedes the motivation state of reactance (see Ratcliff, 2021).

References

Asch, Solomon E. 1951. "Effects of Group Pressure upon the Modification and Distortion of Judgments." In *Groups, Leadership, and Men*, edited by Harold Guetzkow, 177–90. Oxford: Carnegie Press.

Bennion, Elizabeth A., and David W. Nickerson. 2016. "I Will Register and Vote, If You Teach Me How: A Field Experiment Testing Voter Registration in College Classrooms." *PS: Political Science & Politics* 49 (4):867–71. doi: 10.1017/S1049096516001360.

Bennion, Elizabeth, and David Nickerson. 2019. "What We Know about How to Mobilize College Students to Vote." *APSA Preprints*. doi: 10.33774/apsa-2019-t0f6g.

Bhatti, Yosef, Jens Olav Dahlgaard, Jonas Hedegaard Hansen, and Kasper M. Hansen. 2017. "Moving the Campaign from the Front Door to the Front Pocket: Field Experimental Evidence on the Effect of Phrasing and Timing of Text Messages on Voter Turnout." *Journal of Elections, Public Opinion and Parties* 27 (3):291–310. doi: 10.1080/17457289.2016.1270288.

Biggers, Daniel R. 2021. "Can the Backlash against Voter ID Laws Activate Minority Voters? Experimental Evidence Examining Voter Mobilization through Psychological Reactance." *Political Behavior*. 43:1161–1179. doi: 10.1007/s11109-019-09587-0.

Brehm, JackW 1966. *A Theory of Psychological Reactance*. New York: Academic Press.

Brehm, SharonS, and JackW Brehm. 1981. *Psychological Reactance: A Theory of Freedom and Control*. San Diego: Academic Press.

Bryant, Lisa A., Michael J. Hanmer, Alauna C. Safarpour, and Jared McDonald. 2022. "The Power of the State: How Postcards from the State Increased Registration and Turnout in Pennsylvania." *Political Behavior* 1–15. doi: 10.1007/s11109-020-09625-2.

Burden, Barry C., David T. Canon, Kenneth R. Mayer, and Donald P. Moynihan. 2014. "Election Laws, Mobilization, and Turnout: The Unanticipated Consequences of Election Reform." *American Journal of Political Science* 58 (1):95–109. doi: 10.1111/ajps.12063.

Cacioppo, John T., Wendi L. Gardner, and Gary G. Berntson. 1997. "Beyond Bipolar Conceptualizations and Measures: The Case of Attitudes and Evaluative Space." *Personality and Social Psychology Review* 1 (1):3–25. doi: 10.1207/s15327957pspr0101_2.

Campo, Shelly, Dominique Brossard, M. Somjen Frazer, Timothy Marchell, Deborah Lewis, and Janis Talbot. 2003. "Are Social Norms Campaigns Really Magic Bullets? Assessing the Effects of Students' Misperceptions on Drinking Behavior." *Health Communication* 15 (4) 481–97. doi: 10.1207/S15327027HC1504_06.

Cho, Hyunyi, and Laura Sands. 2011. "Gain-And Loss-Frame Sun Safety Messages and Psychological Reactance of Adolescents." *Communication Research Reports: CRR* 28 (4):308–17. doi: 10.1080/08824096.2011.616242.

Chung, Adrienne, and Rajiv N. Rimal. 2016. "Social Norms: A Review." *Review of Communication Research* 4:1–28. doi: 10.12840/issn.2255-4165.2016.04.01.008.

Cialdini, Robert B., Raymond R. Reno, and Carl A. Kallgren. 1990. "A Focus Theory of Normative Conduct: Recycling the Concept of Norms to Reduce Littering in Public Places." *Journal of Personality and Social Psychology* 58 (6):1015–26. doi: 10.1037/0022-3514.58.6.1015.

Dillard, James Price, and Lijiang Shen. 2005. "On the Nature of Reactance and Its Role in Persuasive Health Communication." *Communication Monographs* 72 (2):144–68. doi: 10.1080/03637750500111815.

File, Thom 2014. "Young-Adult Voting: An Analysis of Presidential Elections, 1964–2012." *United States Census Bureau.* https://www.census.gov/library/publications/2014/demo/p20-573.html.

File, Thom 2018. "Characteristics of Voters in the Presidential Election of 2016." *United States Census Bureau.* https://www.census.gov/library/publications/2018/demo/p20-582.html.

Fishbein, Martin, and Icek Ajzen. 2010. Predicting and Changing Behavior: The Reasoned Action Approach. New York: Psychology Press.

Gerber, Alan S, and Todd Rogers. 2009. "Descriptive Social Norms and Motivation to Vote: Everybody's Voting and so Should You." *The Journal of Politics* 71 (1):178–91. doi: 10.1017/S0022381608090117.

Gerber, Alan S., Donald P. Green, and Christopher W. Larimer. 2008. "Social Pressure and Voter Turnout: Evidence from a Large-Scale Field Experiment." *American Political Science Review* 102 (1):33–48. doi: 10.1017/S000305540808009X.

Gerber, Alan S., Donald P. Green, and Christopher W. Larimer. 2010. "An Experiment Testing the Relative Effectiveness of Encouraging Voter Participation by Inducing Feelings of Pride or Shame." *Political Behavior* 32 (3):409–22. doi: 10.1007/s11109-010-9110-4.

Gerber, Alan S., Gregory A. Huber, Albert H. Fang, and Andrew Gooch. 2017. "The Generalizability of Social Pressure Effects on Turnout across High-Salience Electoral Contexts: Field Experimental Evidence from 1.96 Million Citizens in 17 States." *American Politics Research* 45 (4):533–59. doi: 10.1177/1532673X16686556.

Gerber, Alan S., Gregory A. Huber, Albert H. Fang, and Catlan E. Reardon. 2018. "The Comparative Effectiveness on Turnout of Positively versus Negatively Framed Descriptive Norms in Mobilization Campaigns." *American Politics Research* 46 (6):996–1011. doi: 10.1177/1532673X18772276.

Green, Donald P., Mary C. McGrath, and Peter M. Aronow. 2013. "Field Experiments and the Study of Voter Turnout." *Journal of Elections, Public Opinion and Parties* 23 (1):27–48. doi: 10.1080/17457289.2012.728223.

Green, DonaldP, and AlanS Gerber. 2019. *Get out the Vote: How to Increase Voter Turnout.* 4th ed. Washington, DC: Brookings Institution Press.

Haenschen, Katherine, and Jay Jennings. 2019. "Mobilizing Millennial Voters with Targeted Internet Advertisements: A Field Experiment." *Political Communication* 36 (3):357–75. doi: 10.1080/10584609.2018.1548530.

Hassell, Hans J. G, and Emily E. Wyler. 2019. "Negative Descriptive Social Norms and Political Action: People Aren't Acting, so You Should." *Political Behavior* 41 (1):231–56. doi: 10.1007/s11109-018-9450-z.

Holbert, RLance, and MichaelT Stephenson. 2008. "Commentary on the Uses and Misuses of Structural Equation Modeling in Communication Research." In *The SAGE Sourcebook of Advanced Data Analysis Methods for Communication Researchers,* edited by R. Lance Holbert and Michael T. Stephenson, 185–218. Thousand Oaks, CA: Sage.

Kahneman, Daniel, and Amos Tversky. 1979. "Prospect Theory: An Analysis of Decision under Risk." *Econometrica* 47 (2):263–91. doi: 10.2307/1914185.

Kahneman, Daniel, Jack L. Knetsch, and Richard H. Thaler. 1990. "Experimental Tests of the Endowment Effect and the Coase Theorem." *Journal of Political Economy* 98 (6):1325–48. doi: 10.1086/261737.

Keane, Lauren Deschamps, and David W. Nickerson. 2015. "When Reports Depress Rather than Inspire: A Field Experiment Using Age Cohorts as Reference Groups." *Journal of Political Marketing* 14 (4):381–90. doi: 10.1080/15377857.2015.1086129.

Kline, RexB 2016. *Principles and Practice of Structural Equation Modeling.* 4th ed. New York: Guilford Press.

Lapinski, Maria Knight, and Rajiv N. Rimal. 2005. "An Explication of Social Norms." *Communication Theory* 15 (2):127–47. doi: 10.1111/j.1468-2885.2005.tb00329.x.

Lee, Hyunmin, and Glen T. Cameron. 2017. "Utilizing Audiovisual and Gain-Framed Messages to Attenuate Psychological Reactance toward Weight Management Health Messages." *Health Communication* 32 (1):72–81. doi: 10.1080/10410236.2015.1099506.

Mann, Christopher B, and Lisa A. Bryant. 2020. "If You Ask, They Will Come (to Register and Vote): Field Experiments with State Election Agencies on Encouraging Voter Registration." *Electoral Studies* 63:102021. doi: 10.1016/j.electstud.2019.02.012.

Mann, Christopher B. 2010. "Is There Backlash to Social Pressure? A Large-Scale Field Experiment on Voter Mobilization." *Political Behavior* 32 (3):387–407. doi: 10.1007/s11109-010-9124-y.

Mann, Christopher B., Kevin Arceneaux, and David W. Nickerson. 2020. "Do Negatively Framed Messages Motivate Political Participation? Evidence from Four Field Experiments." *American Politics Research* 48 (1):3–21. doi: 10.1177/1532673X19840732.

Matland, Richard E, and Gregg R. Murray. 2013. "An Experimental Test for 'Backlash' against Social Pressure Techniques Used to Mobilize Voters." *American Politics Research* 41 (3):359–85. doi: 10.1177/1532673X12463423.

Miller, Dale T, and Deborah A. Prentice. 2016. "Changing Norms to Change Behavior." *Annual Review of Psychology* 67:339–61. doi: 10.1146/annurev-psych-010814-015013.

Miller, Joanne M, and Jon A. Krosnick. 2004. "Threat as a Motivator of Political Activism: A Field Experiment." *Political Psychology* 25 (4):507–23. doi: 10.1111/j.1467-9221.2004.00384.x.

Murray, Gregg R, and Richard E. Matland. 2014. "Mobilization Effects Using Mail: Social Pressure, Descriptive Norms, and Timing." *Political Research Quarterly* 67 (2):304–19. doi: 10.1177/1065912913499234.

Nan, Xiaoli, Kelly Daily, and Yan Qin. 2018. "Relative Persuasiveness of Gain-Vs. Loss-Framed Messages: A Review of Theoretical Perspectives and Developing an Integrative Framework." *Review of Communication* 18 (4):370–90. doi: 10.1080/15358593.2018.1519845.

Neiheisel, Jacob R, and Barry C. Burden. 2012. "The Impact of Election Day Registration on Voter Turnout and Election Outcomes." *American Politics Research* 40 (4):636–64. doi: 10.1177/1532673X11432470.

O'Keefe, Daniel J, and Jakob D. Jensen. 2006. "The Advantages of Compliance or the Disadvantages of Noncompliance? A Meta-Analytic Review of the Relative Persuasive Effectiveness of Gain-Framed and Loss-Framed Messages." *Annals of the International Communication Association* 30 (1):1–43. doi: 10.1080/23808985.2006.11679054.

O'Keefe, Daniel J, and Jakob D. Jensen. 2007. "The Relative Persuasiveness of Gain-Framed and Loss-Framed Messages for Encouraging Disease Prevention Behaviors: A Meta-Analytic Review." *Journal of Health Communication* 12 (7):623–44. doi: 10.1080/10810730701615198.

O'Keefe, DanielJames 2012. "From Psychological Theory to Message Design: Lessons from the Story of Gain-Framed and Loss-Framed Persuasive Appeals." In *Health Communication Message Design: Theory and Practice*, edited by Hyunyi Cho, 3–20. Thousand Oaks, CA: Sage.

O'Keefe, Daniel J, and Jakob D. Jensen. 2009. "The Relative Persuasiveness of Gain-Framed and Loss-Framed Messages for Encouraging Disease Detection Behaviors: A Meta-Analytic Review." *Journal of Communication* 59 (2):296–316. doi: 10.1111/j.1460-2466.2009.01417.x.

Panagopoulos, Costas 2010. "Affect, Social Pressure and Prosocial Motivation: Field Experimental Evidence of the Mobilizing Effects of Pride, Shame and Publicizing Voting Behavior." *Political Behavior* 32 (3):369–86. doi: 10.1007/s11109-010-9114-0.

Panagopoulos, Costas, Christopher W. Larimer, and Meghan Condon. 2014. "Social Pressure, Descriptive Norms, and Voter Mobilization." *Political Behavior* 36 (2):451–69. doi: 10.1007/s11109-013-9234-4.

Perkins, H Wesley., and Alan D Berkowitz. 1986. Perceiving the community norms of alcohol use among students: Some research implications for campus alcohol education programming. *International journal of the Addictions* 21 (9–10):961–976. doi: 10.3109/10826088609077249

Quick, Brian L, and Benjamin R. Bates. 2010. "The Use of Gain-Or Loss-Frame Messages and Efficacy Appeals to Dissuade Excessive Alcohol Consumption among College Students: A Test of Psychological Reactance Theory." *Journal of Health Communication* 15 (6):603–28. doi: 10.1080/10810730.2010.499593.

Quick, Brian L, and Michael T. Stephenson. 2008. "Examining the Role of Trait Reactance and Sensation Seeking on Perceived Threat, State Reactance, and Reactance Restoration." *Human Communication Research* 34 (3):448–76. doi: 10.1111/j.1468-2958.2008.00328.x.

Quick, Brian L., Jennifer A. Kam, Susan E. Morgan, Claudia A. Montero Liberona, and Rebecca A. Smith. 2015. "Prospect Theory, Discrete Emotions, and Freedom Threats: An Extension of Psychological Reactance Theory." *Journal of Communication* 65 (1):40–61. doi: 10.1111/jcom.12134.

Quick, BrianL, Lijiang Shen, and JamesPrice Dillard. 2013. "Reactance Theory and Persuasion." In *The SAGE Handbook of Persuasion: Advances in Theory and Research*. 2nd ed., edited by James Price Dillard and Lijiang Shen, 167–83. Los Angeles: Sage.

Ratcliff, C. L. 2021. "Characterizing Reactance in Communication Research: A Review of Conceptual and Operational Approaches." *Communication Research* 48 (7):1033–1058. doi: 10.1177/0093650219872126.

Rains, Stephen A. 2013. "The Nature of Psychological Reactance Revisited: A Meta-Analytic Review." *Human Communication Research* 39 (1):47–73. doi: 10.1111/j.1468-2958.2012.01443.x.

Reinhart, Amber Marie, Heather M. Marshall, Thomas Hugh Feeley, and Frank Tutzauer. 2007. "The Persuasive Effects of Message Framing in Organ Donation: The Mediating Role of Psychological Reactance." *Communication Monographs* 74 (2):229–55. doi: 10.1080/03637750701397098.

Reynolds-Tylus, Tobias 2019. "Psychological Reactance and Persuasive Health Communication: A Review of the Literature." *Frontiers in Communication* 4 (56). doi: 10.3389/fcomm.2019.00056.

Reynolds-Tylus, Tobias, Elisabeth Bigsby, and Brian L. Quick. 2021. "A Comparison of Three Approaches for Measuring Negative Cognitions for Psychological Reactance." *Communication Methods and Measures* 15 (1):43–59. doi: 10.1080/19312458.2020.1810647.

Rosenberg, Benjamin D, and Jason T. Siegel. 2018. "A 50-Year Review of Psychological Reactance Theory: Do Not Read This Article." *Motivation Science* 4 (4):281–300. doi: 10.1037/mot0000091.

Shen, Lijiang 2015. "Antecedents to Psychological Reactance: The Impact of Threat, Message Frame, and Choice." *Health Communication* 30 (10):975–85. doi: 10.1080/10410236.2014.910882.

Sherif, Muzafer 1936. *The Psychology of Social Norms*. New York: Harper.

Taylor, Shelley E. 1991. "Asymmetrical Effects of Positive and Negative Events: The Mobilization-Minimization Hypothesis." *Psychological Bulletin* 110 (1):67–85. doi: 10.1037/0033-2909.110.1.67.

Zhao, Xiaoquan, and Xiaoli Nan. 2010. "Influence of Self-Affirmation on Responses to Gain-Versus Loss-Framed Antismoking Messages." *Human Communication Research* 36 (4):493–511. doi: 10.1111/j.1468-2958.2010.01385.x.

Candidate Evaluations and Social Media Following during the 2020 Presidential Campaign

Kate Kenski (iD), Dam Hee Kim (iD), and S. Mo Jones-Jang (iD)

ABSTRACT

This study investigates the relationship between presidential candidate evaluations and following the candidates on five social media (SM) platforms: Facebook, Twitter, Instagram, Snapchat, and YouTube. Analyses of national survey data collected during the 2020 presidential campaign (N = 2,120) suggest that following a candidate on SM is positively associated with feelings toward that candidate, even after gender, age, race, education, party identification, and online news media use have been taken into consideration. Specifically, individuals who followed Trump on Facebook, Twitter, and/or YouTube supported him more than did those who did not follow him. Following Biden on Facebook, Twitter, Instagram, and/or Snapchat was positively associated with his feeling thermometer ratings after demographic variables, party identification, and online news media use were controlled. Moreover, we show that these positive relationships were more pronounced among those who did not identify with one of the major political parties. Following a candidate, however, was not necessarily associated with decreased support for the opposing candidate. Overall, our results highlight the importance of politicians' use of social media during campaigns and suggest that following candidates on different SM platforms has unique relationships with candidate evaluations.

On January 6, 2021, a group of Trump supporters entered the U.S. Capitol in an effort to halt the certification of the 2020 presidential election results. Many of the protesters had come from the "Stop The Steal" rally where Trump told them that "We're gathered together in the heart of our nation's capital for one very, very basic and simple reason: To save our democracy." According to *New York Times* writers Charlie Warzel and Stuart A. Thompson, "About 40 percent of the phones tracked near the rally stage on the National Mall during the speeches were also found in and around the Capitol during the siege — a clear link between those who'd listened to the president and his allies and then marched on the building" (2021). Facebook CEO Mark Zuckerberg banned Trump's account for 24 hours that day, which then turned into a longer suspension (Byers 2021). On January 8, 2021, Twitter announced, "After close review of recent Tweets from the @realDonaldTrump account and the context around them we have permanently suspended the account due to the risk of further incitement of violence" (Fung 2021). An assumption behind his ban from Facebook and Twitter was that exposure to his social media (SM) messaging had the capacity to influence people's attitudes. In this study, we test that assumption by looking at the relationship between following the candidate handles/accounts on SM and candidate evaluations using data collected during the last two weeks of the general election campaign period. Our findings suggest that following candidates on SM and candidate evaluations are positively associated even after political party identification is taken into consideration.

Social media influence

Social media have become prominent communication tools for politicians during election campaigns (Ceron 2017; Stier et al. 2018). The use of Twitter and Facebook among national-level politicians in the U.S. has now reached a near saturation point (Tromble 2018). Social media platforms allow politicians to reach a wide audience and communicate with voters directly (Vergeer 2013). In so doing, candidates construct a public persona and foster intimacy with the electorate (McGregor 2018). The primary goal of candidates' SM use is to appeal to their supporters and to promote their political frames and agendas to the general public and journalists (Kreiss 2016; Kruikemeier, Gattermann, and Vliegenthart 2018). Notably, using Twitter, Donald Trump broadcasted his messages to attract public attention to his campaign agendas during his election campaign (Wells et al. 2016). He used his SM accounts as his bully pulpit although other politicians take a similar strategic approach (Gross and Johnson 2016; Kenski, Filer, and Conway-Silva 2018). Sharing his campaign trails and emotional reactions in a real-time, Trump made his supporters feel as if they attended campaign events with him (McLaughlin and Macafee 2019).

Optimistically, politicians' use of SM helps improve transparency and accountability (Ceron 2017). Bypassing traditional screening and potential journalistic biases, politicians, especially those who have fewer resources than do their political competitors, now have direct dialogue with citizens at a low cost. Citizens may have additional opportunities to compare the actors' actual and declared behaviors on SM. Despite the potential for two-way interaction, however, online relationships between citizens and politicians remain mostly asymmetrical, following a traditional top-down approach (Stromer-Galley 2014). Broadcasting messages rather than conversing with citizens, politicians treat citizens more as followers than as friends. Furthermore, scholars have expressed concerns that SM discussions in a homogeneous network often reinforce or radicalize the users' position, creating an ideologically segregated echo chamber or filter bubble (Pariser 2011).

As politicians have become active on SM, it has become increasingly common for individuals to follow them on SM. In the context of 2016 election, 24% of American adults followed Trump and/or Clinton on SM (Pew Research Center 2016). Before his account was banned in January 2021, Trump had 88 million followers on Twitter while Biden's personal Twitter account had 28.6 million followers in February 2021 (Murdock 2021).

Research demonstrates that partisans tend to prefer news content that aligns with their political views (Iyengar and Hahn 2009; Stroud 2008). It is, therefore, likely that partisans would also be more likely to follow candidates who are from their political party on SM. An October 15, 2020 Pew Research Center report found that popular political Twitter accounts were more likely to be followed by Twitter users who matched the account's party affiliation. For example, @realDonaldTrump was more likely to be followed by Republicans than Democrats and @JoeBiden was more likely to be followed by Democrats than Republicans. In an effort to replicate these findings, therefore, we predict that party identification shaped whether or not someone was likely to follow a particular presidential candidate on SM.

H1a. Republicans were more likely to follow Republican presidential candidate Donald Trump on SM than were non-Republicans.

H1b. Democrats were more likely to follow Democratic presidential candidate Joe Biden on SM than were non-Democrats.

In light of calls for cross-platform research (Hall et al. 2018; Kim and Ellison 2021), we also were curious about the extent to which these expectations held across five SM platforms:

Facebook, Twitter, Instagram, Snapchat, and YouTube. Both general SM following indices for each candidate and following candidates on individual SM platforms were examined in this study.

Beyond party identification and sociodemographic characteristics, we suspect that following a political candidate will positively predict support for that candidate for both cognitive and emotional reasons. For one, following a candidate allows individuals to identify with the candidate, and specifically, to adopt the candidate's cognitive perspective to further support the candidate (McLaughlin and Macafee 2019). Social media allow candidates to bypass news media and share their versions of political reality and campaign directly with followers (Kreiss 2016; Metz, Kruikemeier, and Lecheler 2020). As followers gradually adopt a candidate's political perspective, they want the candidate to win the election. Also, political candidates often use *emotional* appeals on SM in an effort to push their political agenda, attack their opponents, and garner support (Borah 2016; Metz, Kruikemeier, and Lecheler 2020). Indeed, individuals who followed politicians on Facebook and Twitter show stronger emotional reactions, namely enthusiasm about the supported candidate (Weeks et al. 2019). Accordingly, we predict that following a presidential candidate on SM will positively predict that candidate's evaluations.

H2a. Following Donald Trump on SM was positively associated with Trump candidate evaluations.

H2b. Following Joe Biden on SM was positively associated with Biden candidate evaluations.

Following a candidate may also be associated with decreased support for the opposing candidate for the abovementioned cognitive and emotional reasons. McLaughlin and Macafee (2019) found that following a candidate (either Trump or Clinton) on SM was indirectly linked to decreased support for the opposing candidate. Following a politician has been linked to anger directed at the opposing candidate on Facebook, although Weeks et al. (2019) did not find that the link was found on Twitter. We advance the general hypothesis that following a candidate on SM was negatively associated with candidate evaluations of his opposition.

H3a: Following Biden on SM was negatively associated with Trump's candidate evaluations.

H3b: Following Trump on SM was negatively associated with Biden's candidate evaluations.

Partisanship has been shown to be negatively associated with change in candidate assessments during campaigns (Tucker and Smith 2021). Those who do not exhibit strong partisanship at the beginning of a campaign are more likely to change their degrees of support for a candidate based on what they have learned during a campaign. Presumably, independents and those who do not know whether they identify with one of the parties should be more persuadable than those who are Republicans or Democrats. Some scholars, however, argue that independents are latent partisans (Keith et al. 1992). Klar and Krupnikov (2016) contend that independents are not less engaged but feel that partisan labels are negative and, hence, go undercover from those identities. Yet, if SM following is an effective tool for cultivating support, it should activate those who identify as nonpartisans to have stronger positive candidate preferences with those candidates with whom they are following on SM. We hypothesize that:

H4: Not identifying with a specific political party moderated the candidate SM following and candidate evaluation relationship. Those who did not affiliate with a specific party experienced a greater SM effect on candidate evaluations than did those who affiliated with the major parties.

Our exploration into the relationship between following candidates on SM and candidate evaluations is important because candidates have expanded their voter outreach on SM and the number of voters using SM has increased, meriting investigation. Moreover, this study not only looks at SM following in a summative fashion, but it also follows calls-to-action by researchers who have observed that different SM platforms tend to reach different audiences and exhibit different affordances, which is important for those trying to harness the power of SM.

Method

Data

Adults in the U.S. completed an online survey between October 19, 2020 and November 3, 2020. Election Day took place on Tuesday, November 3, and all surveys were completed by 8:50 a.m. that morning. The data were collected through a research company, Dynata. As an online survey, the sample is a non-probability sample. Research examining non-probability and representative samples respectively reports that political results are largely the same (Berinsky, Huber, and Lenz 2012), mitigating to some extent concerns about generalizability. Quotas were applied for age, gender, race and region of the country to ensure that the sample more closely resembled the American population. There were 2,120 participants.

The mean age of respondents was 51.5 years ($SD = 16.1$). There were 46.6% males, 53.0% females, and 0.4% who identified as other. In terms of race, 76.9% self-identified as White, 10.7% self-identified as Black or African American, 6.5% self-identified as Hispanic or Latino, 8.8% self-identified as Asian, 1.7% self-identified as American Indian or Alaska Native, and 0.2% self-identified as Native Hawaiian or Other Pacific Islander. Of all participants, 21.7% came from the West, 22.8% said they were from the East, 21.7% said Midwest, and 33.7% reported coming from the South. In terms of party identification, 34.7% self-identified as Republican, 36.4% said Democrat, 24.6% said independent, 1.7% said "other," and 2.5% did not know how they identified politically.

Dependent variables

Feeling Thermometer toward Trump: Using a sliding scale centered at 5, respondents were asked, "On a scale from 0 to 10, how favorable do you feel toward the presidential candidates?" with "Donald Trump" as the evaluation object (0 = very unfavorable, 10 = very favorable). The average Trump evaluation was 4.15 (SD = 4.14).

Feeling Thermometer toward Biden: Using a sliding scale centered at 5, respondents were asked, "On a scale from 0 to 10, how favorable do you feel toward the presidential candidates?" with "Joe Biden" as the evaluation object (0 = very unfavorable, 10 = very favorable). The average Biden evaluation was 5.00 (SD = 3.92).

Independent variables

Candidate Social Media Following: Study participants were asked "On which social media do you follow Donald Trump? Select all that apply," and, "On which social media do you follow Joe Biden? Select all that apply." Check boxes for Facebook, Twitter, Instagram, Snapchat, and YouTube were offered for each candidate. When asked about following Trump on SM, 18.1% selected Facebook, 15.3% Twitter, 8.9% Instagram, 3.8% Snapchat, and 9.9% YouTube. When asked about following Biden on SM, 14.2% selected Facebook, 12.3% Twitter, 8.7% Instagram, 3.5% Snapchat, and 8.9% YouTube.

Summative SM indices were also created for each candidate by tallying SM following on the five platforms. These indices ranged from 0 to 5. On average, participants followed 0.56 SM platforms for Trump (SD = 1.11) and 0.48 platforms for Biden (SD = 1.03).

Moderating variable: Party affiliation

Political affiliation was measured with the question, "Generally speaking, do you usually think of yourself as a Republican, a Democrat, an Independent, Other (please specify), or Don't know?" Those who identified as an independent or said "don't know" were coded as 1 and those identifying with a political party were coded as 0. This dummy variable was multiplied by the SM following variables to determine whether or not the effects of candidate SM following were more pronounced for those who did not identify with a formal political party.

Control variables

We controlled for five demographic variables, party identification, and online media exposure to liberal and conservative media sources. For demographic control variables, we included age (in years), gender (male = 1, female/other = 0), education (approximation of years), and household income (ordinal scale converted to approximation of dollars in thousands).

Respondents were asked, "Which online sources did you use to get news about politics and the election? Please check any that you used at least once in the past 14 days." Options included *Huffington Post* and/or *Politico*; *Washington Post* and/or *Buzzfeed*; *Breibart, Conservative Tribune* and/or *Drudge Report*; and *Western Journalism, InfoWar, TheBlaze* and/or *WorldNetDaily*. Of respondents, 18.9% reported seeing news about politics and the election on *Huffington Post* and/or *Politico*, 24.4% checked *Washington Post* and/or *Buzzfeed*, 6.8% *Breitbart, Conservative Tribune* and/or *Drudge Report*, and 6.7% *Western Journalism, InfoWar, TheBlaze* and/or *WorldNetDaily*.

Results

The first hypothesis set maintained that partisans would be more likely to follow the presidential candidate from their party than would others, meaning that Republicans would be more likely to follow Trump on SM than Democrats or nonpartisans (H1a) and that Democrats would be more likely to follow Biden on SM than Republicans or nonpartisans (H1b). One-way between subjects ANOVAs were conducted to compare the effect of party identification on the number of SM platforms used to follow Trump and Biden. There were significant effects of party identification on the number of SM used to follow Trump, $F(2, 2,081) = 116.99$, $p < 0.001$ and to follow Biden, $F(2, 2,081) = 30.86$, $p < 0.001$. Post-hoc analyses using the Scheffé post-hoc criterion for significance indicated that the mean score for following Trump on SM platforms was significantly higher for Republicans (M = 1.02, SD = 1.37) than for Democrats (M = 0.38, SD = 0.94) or those unaffiliated with a party (M = 0.24, SD = 0.69) at the $p < 0.001$ level, supporting H1a. For following Biden on SM, Democrats had a higher platform average (M = 0.67, SD = 1.15) than did Republicans (M = 0.49, SD = 1.12) at the $p < 0.01$ level and those unaffiliated with a party (M = 0.22, SD = 0.65) at the $p < 0.001$ level, supporting H1b. There was no statistical difference in following Trump on SM for Democrats and those unaffiliated with a party, but Republicans were more likely to follow Biden than were those unaffiliated with a party at the $p < 0.001$ level.

Chi-square tests were used to see if patterns of SM following differed between the groups. As shown in Table 1, Republicans were more likely to follow Trump on all five SM platforms analyzed than were Democrats or independents/those not sure of their party identification, supporting H1a. Republicans had higher Trump following percentages than did others on Facebook ($\chi^2 = 235.18$, df = 2, $p < 0.001$), Twitter ($\chi^2 = 86.61$, df = 2, $p <0.001$), Instagram ($\chi^2 = 80.50$, df = 2, $p <0.001$), Snapchat ($\chi^2 = 31.83$, df = 2, $p <0.001$), and YouTube ($\chi^2 = 61.24$, df = 2, $p < 0.001$). In each case, the Republicans had twice as high or more of a percentage following the platform than did others. Democrats were more likely to follow Biden on all five SM platforms analyzed than were Republicans or nonpartisans, supporting H1b. Democrats had higher Biden following percentages than did others on Facebook ($\chi^2 = 37.48$, df = 2,

POLITICAL MARKETING AND THE ELECTION OF 2020

Table 1. Percentage of Republicans, Democrats, and Nonpartisans following candidates on five social media platforms.

		Following Trump				Following Biden		
	Rep	Dem	Ind/DK		Rep	Dem	Ind/DK	
Facebook	36.0%	9.8%	7.5%	χ^2 =235.18, df = 2, p<.001	13.2%	19.9%	8.3%	χ^2 =37.48, df = 2, p<.001
Twitter	25.3%	11.8%	8.0%	χ^2 =86.61, df = 2, p<.001	10.9%	19.0%	5.2%	χ^2 =60.64, df = 2, p<.001
Instagram	16.6%	6.1%	3.5%	χ^2 =80.50, df = 2, p<.001	9.8%	11.9%	3.1%	χ^2 =33.57, df = 2, p<.001
Snapchat	6.9%	2.8%	1.2%	χ^2 =31.83, df = 2, p<.001	5.3%	3.5%	1.6%	χ^2 =13.04, df = 2, p<.01
YouTube	17.0%	7.1%	5.2%	χ^2 =61.24, df = 2, p<.001	9.4%	12.3%	4.3%	χ^2 =26.48, df = 2, p<.001

Table 2. Means of Trump and Biden feeling thermometer ratings by following candidates on five social media platforms.

	Trump Feeling Thermometer					Biden Feeling Thermometer				
	Following		Not Following			Following		Not Following		
	Mean	SD	Mean	SD		Mean	SD	Mean	SD	
Trump										
Facebook	7.55	3.26	3.40	3.94	***	4.05	3.95	5.21	3.88	***
Twitter	6.79	3.56	3.68	4.06	***	5.02	3.91	5.00	3.92	
Instagram	7.46	3.22	3.83	4.08	***	5.03	3.91	5.00	3.92	
Snapchat	7.91	2.62	4.01	4.12	***	5.96	3.76	4.96	3.92	*
YouTube	7.20	3.32	3.82	4.09	***	5.35	3.93	4.96	3.92	
Biden										
Facebook	4.11	4.10	4.16	4.15		7.46	3.12	4.59	3.89	***
Twitter	4.13	4.13	4.16	4.15		7.62	2.96	4.63	3.90	***
Instagram	5.19	4.13	4.06	4.13	***	7.48	2.94	4.76	3.92	***
Snapchat	6.59	3.67	4.07	4.14	***	7.67	2.99	4.90	3.92	***
YouTube	5.17	3.93	4.05	4.15	***	7.13	3.29	4.79	3.91	***

$p < 0.001$), Twitter ($\chi^2 = 60.64$, df = 2, $p < 0.001$), Instagram ($\chi^2 = 33.57$, df = 2, $p < 0.001$), Snapchat ($\chi^2 = 13.04$, df = 2, $p <0.001$), and YouTube ($\chi^2 = 26.48$, df = 2, $p < 0.001$).

When chi-square tests were restricted to the differences between Republicans and Democrats (excluding independents/those not sure of their party identification from the analysis), the differences were significantly different across all five of the SM platforms for Trump ($p < 0.001$), but the partisan group differences were only significant for Biden ($p < 0.001$) on the two most used SM platforms, Facebook and Twitter. Partisan differences between Democrats and Republicans were not detected for following Biden on Instagram, Snapchat, or YouTube.

The second hypothesis set contended that candidate evaluations would be associated positively with following candidates on SM platforms. H2a focused on Trump, and H2b focused on Biden. The summative SM following index for Trump was positively associated with his candidate evaluations ($r = 0.38$, $p < 0.001$). Biden's SM following index was also positively associated with his candidate evaluations ($r = 0.29$, $p < 0.001$). Both H2a and H2b were supported by independent samples t tests as well. As shown in Table 2, those who followed Trump on Facebook, $t(654.43) = 21.69$, $p < 0.001$, Twitter, $t(487.70) = 14.15$, $p < 0.001$, Instagram, $t(251.27) = 14.38$, $p < 0.001$, Snapchat, $t(95.13) = 12.75$, $p < 0.001$, and/or YouTube, $t(285.66) = 13.70$, $p < 0.001$ gave him higher evaluations on the feeling thermometer than did those who did not follow him on the platforms. Levene's test indicated that the null hypotheses of equal variances were rejected for following Trump on Facebook, $F(1, 2,118) = 104.86$, $p < 0.001$, Twitter, $F(1, 2,118) = 56.76$, $p < 0.001$, Instagram, $F(1, 2,118) = 93.27$, $p < 0.001$, Snapchat, $F(1, 2,118) = 100.38$, $p < 0.001$, and YouTube, $F(1, 2,118) = 83.06$, $p < 0.001$. The t tests for those groups were adjusted accordingly. Using a Bonferroni-corrected p-value, to be considered statistically significant the p-values would need to be less than 0.01. In all cases, the values were significant by this threshold.

Those who followed Biden on Facebook, $t(469.06) = 14.20$, $p < 0.001$, Twitter, $t(396.55) = 14.58$, $p < 0.001$, Instagram, $t(249.37) = 11.59$, $p < 0.001$, Snapchat, $t(83.60) = 7.78$, $p < 0.001$), and/or YouTube, $t(243.19) = 9.15$, $p < 0.001$) gave him higher evaluations on the feeling thermometer than did those who did not follow him. Levene's test indicated that the null hypotheses of equal variances were rejected for following Biden on Facebook, $F(1, 2,118) = 97.82$, $p < 0.001$, Twitter, $F(1, 2,118) = 131.93$, $p < 0.001$, Instagram, $F(1, 2,118) = 90.79$, $p < 0.001$, Snapchat, $F(1, 2,118) = 33.25$, $p < 0.001$, and YouTube, $F(1, 2,118) = 43.61$, $p < 0.001$. Again, using the Bonferroni-corrected p-value of less than 0.01, all give platforms met the threshold of statistical significance.

To further test H2a and H2b, ordinary least square regressions were run predicting candidate feeling thermometer scores from the candidate SM following variables controlling for age, gender, race, education, household income, party identification, and online news media use of four media outlets (two liberal source items, two conservative source items). As shown in the first model in Table 3, following Trump on Facebook ($ß = 0.15$, $p < 0.001$), Twitter ($ß = 0.10$, $p < 0.001$), and/YouTube ($ß = 0.04$, $p < 0.05$) was positively associated with his feeling thermometer ratings. Following Trump on Instagram and Snapchat did not affect his ratings. The multivariate results supported H2a for three of five SM platforms. Table 4 shows the results for following Biden on SM on his feeling thermometer ratings. H2b was supported for four of five SM platforms: Facebook ($ß = 0.14$, $p < 0.001$), Twitter ($ß = 0.10$, $p < 0.001$), Instagram ($ß = 0.05$, $p < 0.05$), and/or Snapchat ($ß = 0.05$, $p < 0.01$). Overall, the results indicate that following candidates on SM is positively associated with people's evaluations of them, even controlling for demographic variables, party identification, and online media use of liberal and conservative sources.

The third hypothesis stated that a candidate's opposition was affected by following a candidate on SM platforms. The results are mixed at both the bivariate and multivariate levels. The summative SM following index for Biden was positively but weakly associated with Trump's candidate evaluations ($r = 0.06$, $p < 0.01$). Trump's SM following index was not associated with Biden's candidate evaluations ($r = -0.02$, $p = 0.311$). As shown in Table 2, people who followed Biden on SM reported higher evaluations of Trump than did those who did not follow Biden when it came to following Biden on Instagram, Snapchat, and YouTube at the bivariate level. People following Trump on Facebook had lower evaluations of Biden than did those who did not follow Trump, and people following Trump on Snapchat reporter higher evaluations of Biden than did those who did not follow Trump on SM at the bivariate level. The mixed and somewhat counterintuitive findings may indicate that those who were invested in politics and with partisan leanings were more likely to be the ones following both candidates. As noted previously, opposition party members were more likely to follow the opposition candidate than were nonpartisans. A more robust test of the relationships takes into account demographic characteristics and party identification.

As shown in Table 3, once partisanship was controlled following Biden on SM had no association with Trump's feeling thermometer evaluations, except for Facebook ($ß = -0.08$, $p < 0.001$) and Twitter ($ß = -0.04$, $p < 0.05$) where the associations were negative. Once partisanship was controlled following Trump had no association with Biden's evaluations, except for Facebook ($ß = -0.06$, $p < 0.01$) and YouTube ($ß = 0.05$, $p < 0.05$) as shown in Table 4. For those who followed Trump on Facebook, Biden's evaluations were lower than for those who did not follow him on that platform. For those who followed Trump on YouTube, however, Biden's ratings went up. In sum, for the most part, following a candidate's opponent on SM had no association with that candidate's ratings. In the three of four situations in which significant findings appeared, following an opponent on SM had a negative association with a candidate's feeling thermometer evaluations. Overall H3 was not supported.

The fourth hypothesis maintained that those who were not affiliated with political parties would be more influenced by following candidates on SM. To test this hypothesis, interactions between SM following and identifying as independent or saying that one didn't know how to identify were added to the models. For the Trump feeling thermometer evaluation, the

Table 3. OLS regressions predicting Trump feeling thermometer evaluations.

	Model 1				Model 2			
	B	SE	Beta		B	SE	Beta	
Intercept	4.43	0.49		***	4.40	0.49		***
Age (in years)	0.00	0.00	0.01		0.00	0.00	0.01	
Male (=1, female/other = 0)	0.17	0.13	0.02		0.13	0.13	0.02	
White (=1, else = 0)	0.17	0.15	0.02		0.18	0.15	0.02	
Education (in years)	−0.10	0.03	−0.05	**	−0.10	0.03	−0.05	**
Household income (in thousands)	0.00	0.00	−0.01		0.00	0.00	−0.01	
Republican (=1, else = 0)	3.64	0.17	0.42	***	3.80	0.18	0.44	***
Democrat (=1, else = 0)	−1.75	0.16	−0.20	***	−1.77	0.17	−0.21	***
Huffington Post and/or Politico (yes = 1, no = 0)	−0.63	0.18	−0.06	***	−0.68	0.18	−0.06	***
Washington Post and/or Buzzfeed (yes = 1, no = 0)	−0.58	0.16	−0.06	***	−0.53	0.16	−0.06	**
Breibart, Conservative Tribune, and/or Drudge Report (yes = 1, no = 0)	1.24	0.26	0.08	***	1.18	0.26	0.07	***
Western Journalism, InfoWar, TheBlaze and/or WorldNetDaily (yes = 1, no = 0)	1.16	0.29	0.07	***	1.33	0.29	0.08	***
Social Media Following								
Trump Facebook (yes = 1, no = 0)	1.65	0.21	0.15	***	1.37	0.22	0.13	***
Trump Twitter (yes = 1, no = 0)	1.16	0.22	0.10	***	0.91	0.24	0.08	***
Trump Instagram (yes = 1, no = 0)	0.23	0.31	0.02		0.00	0.32	0.00	
Trump Snapchat (yes = 1, no = 0)	0.51	0.41	0.02		0.72	0.43	0.03	
Trump YouTube (yes = 1, no = 0)	0.55	0.28	0.04	*	0.50	0.30	0.04	
Biden Facebook (yes = 1, no = 0)	−0.90	0.22	−0.08	***	−0.64	0.24	−0.05	**
Biden Twitter (yes = 1, no = 0)	−0.50	0.25	−0.04	*	−0.21	0.26	−0.02	
Biden Instagram (yes = 1, no = 0)	0.40	0.30	0.03		0.51	0.32	0.03	
Biden Snapchat (yes = 1, no = 0)	−0.36	0.43	−0.02		−0.67	0.46	−0.03	
Biden YouTube (yes = 1, no = 0)	0.04	0.28	0.00		0.08	0.30	0.01	
Trump Facebook X Ind/DK					2.41	0.61	0.08	***
Trump Twitter X Ind/DK					1.58	0.60	0.06	**
Trump Instagram X Ind/DK					2.89	0.96	0.07	**
Trump Snapchat X Ind/DK					−2.01	1.40	−0.03	
Trump YouTube X Ind/DK					−0.81	0.94	−0.02	
Biden Facebook X Ind/DK					−1.84	0.57	−0.07	**
Biden Twitter X Ind/DK					−2.16	0.70	−0.06	**
Biden Instagram X Ind/DK					−2.06	0.98	−0.05	*
Biden Snapchat X Ind/DK					2.46	1.33	0.04	
Biden YouTube X Ind/DK					−0.17	0.96	0.00	
R-square		0.54				0.55		
N		2,120				2,120		

Table 4. OLS regressions predicting Biden feeling thermometer evaluations.

	Model 1				Model 2			
	B	SE	Beta		B	SE	Beta	
Intercept	1.35	0.48		**	1.37	0.48		**
Age (in years)	0.03	0.00	0.10	***	0.02	0.00	0.10	***
Male (=1, female/other = 0)	−0.07	0.13	−0.01		−0.04	0.13	−0.01	
White (=1, else = 0)	−0.49	0.15	−0.05	**	−0.49	0.15	−0.05	**
Education (in years)	0.11	0.03	0.07	***	0.11	0.03	0.07	***
Household income (in thousands)	0.00	0.00	0.03		0.00	0.00	0.03	
Republican (=1, else = 0)	−2.10	0.17	−0.26	***	−2.20	0.18	−0.27	***
Democrat (=1, else = 0)	3.02	0.16	0.37	***	3.10	0.17	0.38	***
Huffington Post and/or Politico (yes = 1, no = 0)	0.20	0.18	0.02		0.26	0.18	0.03	
Washington Post and/or Buzzfeed (yes = 1, no = 0)	0.74	0.16	0.08	***	0.69	0.16	0.08	***
Breibart, Conservative Tribune, and/or Drudge Report (yes = 1, no = 0)	−0.65	0.26	−0.04	*	−0.59	0.26	−0.04	*
Western Journalism, InfoWar, TheBlaze and/or WorldNetDaily (yes = 1, no = 0)	−0.38	0.29	−0.02		−0.51	0.29	−0.03	
Social Media Following								
Trump Facebook (yes = 1, no = 0)	−0.63	0.21	−0.06	**	−0.45	0.22	−0.04	*
Trump Twitter (yes = 1, no = 0)	−0.03	0.22	0.00		0.23	0.24	0.02	
Trump Instagram (yes = 1, no = 0)	−0.46	0.30	−0.03		−0.30	0.32	−0.02	
Trump Snapchat (yes = 1, no = 0)	0.09	0.41	0.00		0.07	0.43	0.00	
Trump YouTube (yes = 1, no = 0)	0.68	0.28	0.05	*	0.94	0.29	0.07	**
Biden Facebook (yes = 1, no = 0)	1.58	0.22	0.14	***	1.11	0.24	0.10	***
Biden Twitter (yes = 1, no = 0)	1.22	0.24	0.10	***	0.99	0.26	0.08	***
Biden Instagram (yes = 1, no = 0)	0.74	0.30	0.05	*	0.64	0.32	0.05	*
Biden Snapchat (yes = 1, no = 0)	1.13	0.43	0.05	**	1.30	0.46	0.06	**
Biden YouTube (yes = 1, no = 0)	0.32	0.28	0.02		0.30	0.30	0.02	
Trump Facebook X Ind/DK					−1.53	0.60	−0.05	*
Trump Twitter X Ind/DK					−1.49	0.59	−0.06	*
Trump Instagram X Ind/DK					−1.89	0.95	−0.05	*
Trump Snapchat X Ind/DK					−0.98	1.39	−0.01	
Trump YouTube X Ind/DK					−1.78	0.93	−0.05	
Biden Facebook X Ind/DK					2.61	0.57	0.10	***
Biden Twitter X Ind/DK					1.68	0.70	0.05	*
Biden Instagram X Ind/DK					1.93	0.97	0.05	*
Biden Snapchat X Ind/DK					−0.99	1.32	−0.02	
Biden YouTube X Ind/DK					1.40	0.96	0.04	
R-square		0.49				0.50		
N		2,120				2,120		

interactions between independent/don't know identification and following Trump on SM should be positive, and the interactions between independent/don't know identification and following Biden on SM should be negative. For the Biden feeling thermometer evaluation, the interactions between independent/don't know identification and following Trump on SM should be negative, and the interactions between independent/don't know identification and following Biden on SM should be positive. Support for the hypothesis is found in Tables 3 and 4 (Model 2). As shown in Table 3, for predicting Trump evaluations, three of the five following Trump on SM interactions with being independent/don't know are positive and significant, and three of the five following Biden on SM interactions are negative and significant. As shown in Table 4, for predicting Biden evaluations, three of the five following Trump on SM interactions with being independent/don't know are negative and significant, and three of the five following Biden on SM interactions are positive and significant. H4 was supported.

Discussion

This purpose of this study was to examine whether or not following candidates on SM was positively associated with attitudes toward the candidates. As expected, and consistent with previous scholarship, partisans were more likely to follow their party's presidential candidate on SM than were those with other types of affiliations or no affiliation at all. Importantly, the data also indicated that there were significant relationships between SM following and candidate evaluations even after demographic variables, party identification, and online news media use were taken into consideration, suggesting that SM appears to have a relationship unique to candidate evaluations and one that hints at the possibilities of influence. This association appears to be most pronounced for those who are not affiliated with the major parties.

The study used data from an online survey that utilized a quota sampling approach. It is possible that the survey was not completely generalizable, and it is the case that surveys were called into question in 2020 given that they appeared to oversample those who preferred Biden. To mitigate against these concerns, the sample size was robust and controls were put into place to dampen concerns over party preference being a confound.

Another limitation is that the following candidates on SM variables were dichotomous. It is not possible with the data collected to examine how frequency of exposure to candidate posts may have influenced candidate evaluations. We assume that more contact or exposure is likely to be bring about greater influence, but it is beyond the scope of this study to test that assumption.

A third limitation is that this study utilizes cross-sectional data. It is possible that candidate evaluations are driving SM following, but with the controls put in place, there are hints that SM may have the capacity to shape the impressions people have about the candidates, especially with those less invested in the major parties. Future studies ought to tease out the causal direction of the relationships investigated in this research. In an ideal study, we would have multiple waves to test the causal relationship between SM following and candidate evaluations with a large enough sample size and spacing between waves to capture the direction of the influence. The positive associations detected in the face of party identification controls included, however, open the door for future studies to test whether SM following causes voters to increase their evaluations of the candidates whom they are following. We suspect that information about candidates via the SM following shapes evaluations but will leave it to other studies to test this assumption.

An important contribution of this study is that not only did the study produce results consistent with Weeks et al. (2019) regarding positive associations between SM following and candidate evaluations, but it expanded on previous work by testing the associations for individual SM platforms. Practitioners will note that following candidates on SM was limited and that some platforms had smaller appeal than others (e.g., only 3.8% followed Trump on Snapchat and 3.5% followed Biden on Snapchat). Nevertheless, in the multivariate context with many control variables, YouTube was significantly associated with Trump's ratings and Snapchat and Instagram were significantly associated with Biden's ratings even with the larger share SM (i.e., Facebook and Twitter) being positively associated with candidate evaluations as well. In other words, different SM platforms appear to have unique associations with candidate evaluations.

Another contribution of this study is the finding that the SM following and candidate evaluation relationships were stronger for nonpartisans than partisans. Other studies may wish to parse out differences between nonpartisans who identify as independents and those who simply say they don't know how they identify. Regardless of whether one believes nonpartisans are latent partisans or whether they are "pure," the nonpartisanship moderating variable was statistically associated with the stronger SM following/candidate evaluation relationships. Either the SM activated leanings that were already there or they persuaded people about particular candidates. Whatever the mechanism behind the relationship, which will hopefully be uncovered in future studies, the relationship is of importance to students of election campaigns.

ORCID

Kate Kenski (iD) http://orcid.org/0000-0002-6064-791X
Dam Hee Kim (iD) http://orcid.org/0000-0001-6060-6686
S. Mo Jones-Jang (iD) http://orcid.org/0000-0003-3935-7421

References

Berinsky, A. J., G. A. Huber, and G. S. Lenz. 2012. "Evaluating Online Labor Markets for Experimental Research: Amazon.com's Mechanical Turk." *Political Analysis* 20 (3):351–68. doi: 10.1093/pan/mpr057.

Borah, P. 2016. "Political Facebook Use: Campaign Strategies Used in 2008 and 2012 Presidential Elections." *Journal of Information Technology & Politics* 13 (4):326–38. doi: 10.1080/19331681.2016.1163519.

Byers, D. 2021. "How Facebook and Twitter Decided to Take Down Trump's Accounts." January 14. https://www.nbcnews.com/tech/tech-news/how-facebook-twitter-decided-take-down-trump-s-accounts-n1254317

Ceron, A. 2017. *Social Media and Political Accountability: Bridging the Gap between Citizens and Politicians*. New York: Springer.

Fung, B. 2021. "Twitter Bans President Trump Permanently." January 9. https://www.cnn.com/2021/01/08/tech/trump-twitter-ban/index.html

Gross, J. H., and K. T. Johnson. 2016. "Twitter Taunts and Tirades: Negative Campaigning in the Age of Trump." *PS: Political Science & Politics* 49 (04):748–54. doi: 10.1017/S1049096516001700.

Hall, M., A. Mazarakis, M. Chorley, and S. Caton. 2018. "Editorial of the Special Issue on following User Pathways: Key Contributions and Future Directions in Cross-Platform Social Media Research." *International Journal of Human–Computer Interaction* 34 (10):895–912. doi: 10.1080/10447318.2018.1471575.

Iyengar, S., and K. S. Hahn. 2009. "Red Media, Blue Media: Evidence of Ideological Selectivity in Media Use." *Journal of Communication* 59 (1):19–39. doi: 10.1111/j.1460-2466.2008.01402.x.

Keith, B. E., D. B. Magleby, C. J. Nelson, E. Orr, M. C. Westlye, and R. E. Wolfinger. 1992. *The Myth of the Independent Voters*. Berkeley: University of California Press

Kenski, K., C. R. Filer, and B. A. Conway-Silva. 2018. "Lying, Liars, and Lies: Incivility in 2016 Presidential Candidate and Campaign Tweets during the Invisible Primary." *American Behavioral Scientist* 62 (3):286–99. doi: 10.1177/0002764217724840.

Kim, D. H., and N. B. Ellison. 2021. "From Observation on Social Media to Offline Political Participation: The Social Media Affordances Approach." *New Media & Society*:146144482199834. doi: 10.1177/1461444821998346.

Klar, S., and Y. Krupnikov. 2016. *Independent Politics: How American Disdain for Parties Leads to Political Inaction*. Cambridge: Cambridge University Press.

Kreiss, D. 2016. "Seizing the Moment: The Presidential Campaigns' Use of Twitter during the 2012 Electoral Cycle." *New Media & Society* 18 (8):1473–90. doi: 10.1177/1461444814562445.

Kruikemeier, S., K. Gattermann, and R. Vliegenthart. 2018. "Understanding the Dynamics of Politicians' Visibility in Traditional and Social Media." *The Information Society* 34 (4):215–28. doi: 10.1080/01972243.2018.1463334.

McGregor, S. C. 2018. "Personalization, Social Media, and Voting: Effects of Candidate Self-Personalization on Vote Intention." *New Media & Society* 20 (3):1139–60. doi: 10.1177/1461444816686103.

McLaughlin, B., and T. Macafee. 2019. "Becoming a Presidential Candidate: Social Media following and Politician Identification." *Mass Communication and Society* 22 (5):584–603. doi: 10.1080/15205436.2019.1614196.

Metz, M., S. Kruikemeier, and S. Lecheler. 2020. "Personalization of Politics on Facebook: Examining the Content and Effects of Professional, Emotional, and Private Self-Personalization." *Information, Communication & Society* 23 (10):1481–98. doi: 10.1080/1369118X.2019.1581244.

Murdock, J. 2021. "Why Joe Biden Has Millions Fewer Twitter Followers Than Trump Did One Month Into Office." *Newsweek*, February 22. https://www.newsweek.com/joe-biden-donald-trump-potus-account-twitter-follo wers-one-month-presidency-1570950

Pariser, E. 2011. *The Filter Bubble: How the New Personalized Web is Changing What We Read and How We Think*. London, UK: Penguin.

Pew Research Center. 2016. "Election 2016: Campaigns as a Direct Source of News." https://www.journalism. org/2016/07/18/election-2016-campaigns-as-a-direct-source-of-news/

Pew Research Center. 2020. "Differences in How Democrats and Republicans Behave on Twitter." https://www. pewresearch.org/politics/2020/10/15/differences-in-how-democrats-and-republicans-behave-on-twitter/

Stier, S., A. Bleier, H. Lietz, and M. Strohmaier. 2018. "Election Campaigning on Social Media: Politicians, Audiences, and the Mediation of Political Communication on Facebook and Twitter." *Political Communication* 35 (1):50–74. doi: 10.1080/10584609.2017.1334728.

Stromer-Galley, J. 2014. *Presidential Campaigning in the Internet Age*. New York: Oxford University Press.

Stroud, N. J. 2008. "Media Use and Political Predispositions: Revisiting the Concept of Selective Exposure." *Political Behavior* 30 (3):341–66. doi: 10.1007/s11109-007-9050-9.

Tromble, R. 2018. "Thanks for (Actually) Responding! How Citizen Demand Shapes Politicians' Interactive Practices on Twitter." *New Media & Society* 20 (2):676–97. doi: 10.1177/1461444816669158.

Trump, D. 2021. "Trump's January 6, 2021 Speech." *National Public Radio*, January 6. https://www.npr. org/2021/02/10/966396848/read-trumps-jan-6-speech-a-key-part-of-impeachment-trial

Tucker, P. D., and S. S. Smith. 2021. "Changes in Candidate Evaluations over the Campaign Season: A Comparison of House, Senate, and Presidential Races." *Political Behavior* 43 (4):1639–61. doi: 10.1007/s11109-020-09603-8.

Vergeer, M. 2013. "Politics, Elections and Online Campaigns: Past, Present… and a Peek into the Future." *New Media & Society* 15 (1):9–17. doi: 10.1177/1461444812457327.

Warzel, C., and S. A. Thompson. 2021. "They Stormed the Capitol. Their Apps Tracked Them." *New York Times*, February 5. https://www.nytimes.com/2021/02/05/opinion/capitol-attack-cellphone-data.html?fbclid=IwAR3aL-TOajXDMY4aSMq8EINPb66OT04JIIbH7vMhTxA1SRuiII9IxFseBN5Y

Weeks, B. E., D. H. Kim, L. B. Hahn, T. H. Diehl, and N. Kwak. 2019. "Hostile Media Perceptions in the Age of Social Media: Following Politicians, Emotions, and Perceptions of Media Bias." *Journal of Broadcasting & Electronic Media* 63 (3):374–92. doi: 10.1080/08838151.2019.1653069.

Wells, C., D. V. Shah, J. C. Pevehouse, J. Yang, A. Pelled, F. Boehm, J. Lukito, S. Ghosh, and J. L. Schmidt. 2016. "How Trump Drove Coverage to the Nomination: Hybrid Media Campaigning." Political Communication 33 (4):669–76. doi: 10.1080/10584609.2016.1224416.

Afterword: Political Marketing, the 2022 Midterms and Future Campaigns

Bruce I. Newman and Jody C Baumgartner

This volume presented an eclectic analysis of the role that various key political marketing tools played in the 2020 US presidential election. Towner and Muñoz examined how Trump and Biden utilized the "Stories" feature of Instagram to market themselves and engage with users. Evans explored differences in how male and female candidates for the House of Representatives marketed or highlighted various issues on Twitter. Conway and her colleagues focused on intermedia agenda-setting, in particular the balance between Twitter feeds and newspapers during the campaign. Reynolds-Tylus and Schill focused on the consumer side of political marketing, highlighting on the idea that there was little difference in reactions to positively or negatively framed get-out-the-vote messages among college students. Kenski and her colleagues were also interested in how the marketing campaign played out among citizens, showing that following a candidate on social media was associated with positive evaluations of that candidate.

These chapters provide an interesting snapshot of a few key ways in which political marketing and the Internet intersected during the campaign of 2020. Importantly, the collection ignores several key aspects of political marketing and raises other questions. In short, given the fact that the campaign landscape continues to change, this book opens the door to further research.

Background

For the past 20 years we have been witnessing a paradigm shift in electoral politics in the US and around the globe. This shift has involved the use of micro-targeting, social media, and big data in political campaigns, begun in earnest by the Obama campaigns of 2008 and 2012. All three strategic tools were used to target finely tuned messages to critical voting blocs and individual voters in order to prevail in races around the country. Marketing research tools and techniques typically used by commercial organizations were employed with a level of sophistication never before seen in a presidential race (or, for that matter, in a commercial campaign). Relying on data analysis which predicted how key issues, policies, or candidate characteristics would affect voting behavior, Obama's organization (in both races) won over enough citizens to prevail in the Electoral College in key battleground states.

In 2016, Donald Trump relied on methods used by the Obama juggernaut but added a new element. In particular, Trump introduced the political marketplace to the increasingly important role that branding plays in politics. Relying heavily on Twitter, as well as the hat he wore at most campaign stops, Trump hammered home his campaign theme of "Make America Great Again" (MAGA). This brand image consistently reinforced the attitudes of his loyal following. The strategy was, of course, successful, and Trump both won the presidency and effectively took over the Republican Party. Positioning himself as the ultimate outsider, Trump was able to convince enough voters that the country was failing economically, culturally, and in the global arena.

From a political marketing perspective, much of Trump's success was based on the use of communication vehicles that were introduced earlier. While he made use of a number of these, he relied heavily on Twitter. In fact, were it not for the numerous controversies Trump embroiled himself in during the 2016 and 2020 campaigns and his presidency, he might have been remembered as the "Twitter president." His "@realDonaldTrump" account attracted almost 90 million followers before it was suspended in January 2021. This provided him with an unparalleled ability to engage in instant, targeted, and direct marketing with his supporters. Importantly, news coverage of his activity on Twitter extended his reach far beyond direct supporters, which gave him an even greater ability to get his message out and potentially expand his support base.

This brings us to the role of political marketing in the 2020 race. Joe Biden's defeat of Trump reinforced an important dictum in commercial marketing, in particular, that customers stick with or switch to a competitive product or service based on their level of satisfaction with a company's offerings. While one can identify several reasons for why Biden succeeded and Trump failed in 2020, nothing played a greater role than the expectations voters had for each. By 2020, Trump was the ultimate "insider," whose words and actions as president were well covered by traditional media and communicated in a plethora of campaign messages. Ironically, as was the case in 2016, the judgment by voters in 2020 was a result of Trump's brand strategy, one that they ultimately seemed to reject.

The 2022 Election

In 2022, the pundits were wrong again. The expected sweep by the Republican Party (or as some would argue, the Trump Party), the so-called "Red Wave," never materialized. In fact, while the Republicans regained control of the House of Representatives, they did so by the barest of margins, with Democrats losing far fewer seats than expected. In addition, Democrats retained control of the Senate, and of this writing, they may actually gain one seat. It was arguably the best mid-term showing for a presidential party since 2002, when George W. Bush's Republicans gained seats in both the House and the Senate.

These results suggest that the 2008 paradigm shift centered around the increasingly important role of political marketing in US elections is in a continual state of change. So what happened in 2022 that left pollsters and pundits alike attempting to figure out why the Republicans – and by extension, Trump – fell short? Moreover, how will the marketing lessons of the mid-term elections affect the 2024 presidential election?

First of all, a focus and reliance on marketing and promotion will certainly continue. Politics will continue to move away from party-dominated to marketing-dominated issues. Here, we see a focus on policies, stereotypes, personality traits of individual politicians, and other curiosity factors that can capture the attention of voters.

Second, we can expect the continued abdication by parties of the vetting process that used to be key in the nomination process. This will be replaced by the ability of both insiders and outsiders to rely on new media technologies to run against incumbents. With a reliance on the communication practices discussed in this book, used by both winners and losers in 2022, we can expect campaign managers to dissect the communication strategies that proved to be most effective. Of particular importance in this regard, is the ability to raise huge sums of money online. Some estimates suggest better than $9 billion was spent in 2022, $2 billion more than in 2018.

Third, another dictum in commercial marketing is the need to understand your customer and introduce products and services that satisfy their needs and wants. The 2022 election reinforced the importance of not wasting any resources delivering messages and appeals that do not matter to voters. Similar to Bill Clinton's 1992 strategy, in which he demanded a singular focus on the campaign theme of "it's the economy stupid," it was evident in 2022 that candidates who focused on pocketbook issues like the economy and inflation enjoyed a good deal of electoral success. This could lead one to wonder how and why Democratic candidates won, when many voters attributed the bad economy to Biden, informal leader of the party. The answer lies with the fact that there was a more important factor that led voters to choose Democrats over Republicans, in particular, the role that Donald Trump played during the campaign.

A fourth factor in politics is to never lie to the American people. At the very top of the list of personality factors that voters rely on to choose a politician is trust. In the end, the Republican Party was seen as the Trump Party, and candidates that he hand-picked to run in some key races were not perceived as believable or capable to lead their state or the nation. Many of these candidates seemed to buy in to Trump's narrative regarding the illegitimacy of the 2020 presidential vote. Election deniers, as they were called, not only echoed these claims in 2022 but expressed doubt that the 2022 results would be legitimate. Voters appeared to be skeptical of these so-called election deniers.

While Trump's hand-picked candidates were successful in winning their party primaries, they were decidedly less so in the general election. This was perhaps most evident in the highly publicized race between the Democrat John Fetterman and the Republican Mehmet Oz, candidates for the US Senate in Pennsylvania. Other notable losses by Trump choices included Doug Mastriano, candidate for governor also in Pennsylvania, Lee Zeldin, gubernatorial candidate in New York, and Arizona Senate candidate Blake Masters.

Finally, voters were faced with choosing between candidates in both parties who were trying to convince them they had their best interests at heart. To be sure, numerous issues like inflation, the economy, abortion, crime, and immigration, to name a few, played a role in the campaign. But a key marketing challenge for candidates is to make themselves believable, to be seen as someone who cares. This is the ultimate challenge for every political candidate, regardless of the issues at stake. Voters want to be convinced that their leaders will do whatever is necessary to make the country a better, safer, healthier, and more desirable place to live.

This brings us back to the role of promotion and marketing in politics. It is not only the medium that matters, but rather that a message is communicated by a messenger who people trust. It is imperative that marketing research not, by itself, dictate strategy. It is also critical that candidates convey a certain passion about what matters to voters, and their own willingness to follow their hearts rather than polling data.

Final Thoughts: Looking Toward 2024

The chapters in this book have clearly shown that different media are better suited to different kinds of messages and that different kinds of politicians are better suited to different media. The ability to match each individual candidate with a believable message delivered through the appropriate medium is the best strategic approach any politician can take. This takes an enormous amount of coordination within a campaign's organizational hierarchy, particularly if the strategy is to be implemented consistently throughout the campaign. While a crisis may force a campaign to pivot and alter their message somewhat, it cannot diverge from the overall image developed and reinforced over the campaign cycle.

This book reinforces the idea, confirmed in elections over recent presidential cycles, that without an understanding of political marketing (including the role of strategists and pollsters) and the evolving role of political parties and voters, no election can be won. Marketing, especially in the realm of electoral politics, relies on the ability of sophisticated campaigns to forecast the future correctly, put forward candidates who are appealing and trustworthy, and understand what matters to voters.

To the surprise of few, Donald Trump has announced he will run for the presidency in 2024. There is no doubt he will be a formidable candidate, even without the two years he has to resurrect his somewhat tarnished brand image. It remains to be seen how Republican Party leaders respond to his perceived failures in this recent election and whether they hold him accountable for the results. It also remains to be seen whether other candidates in the Republican Party can rise to the challenge to take him on.

One interesting issue to emerge in 2022 was the idea that American democracy itself might increasingly be at stake. This notion, pushed mainly by those on the left, seemed to be an amalgamation of rejecting the claims of election deniers as well as promoting the idea that voter identification laws suppress the vote of minority voters. Thus far the Democrats have had some success in marketing this idea, but it remains to be seen how Republicans will counter it in 2024.

Other critical factors looking forward to 2024 will be how well the economy bounces back and whether there are continued threats by dictators around the world, as well as how President Biden responds to those events. Perhaps even more important will be the role of unexpected events that are impossible to forecast and the ability of the eventual nominees of both parties to respond. The ability of a candidate to maintain grace under the intense spotlight of a campaign is critical. This includes debate performances, which still matter. We live a time when communication vehicles afford any interested voter the opportunity to evaluate every utterance and nuance exhibited by a politician, as the surveillance of campaigns are scrutinized on a 24/7 basis.

Index

Note: Page numbers followed by "n" denote endnotes.

Aaker, D. A. 9
affordances 23–25, 26, 77
Ajzen, Icek 67
Aronow, Peter M. 64
associations 12, 13, 63, 69, 80, 83
attributes 8, 9

Bernhardt, P. 26
Bhatti, Yosef 64
Biden, Joe: campaign 28–33; candidate evaluations 76, 80
Biggers, Daniel R. 62
Bigsby, Elisabeth 67
Bossetta, M. 25, 26
brands 3–6, 8, 9, 11, 12, 14, 15; concept 3, 4, 6, 14, 15; perspectives 3, 4, 11, 15, 16; theories 4

campaigning/campaigns 2, 24–7, 29–31, 33, 34, 38–9, 57, 76, 86, 88, 89; events 25, 27, 32, 33, 75; messages 24, 87; Twitter feeds 2, 51; workers 25, 26, 33
candidate communication 45
candidate evaluations 74, 76, 79, 83, 84; relationships 76, 84
celebrities 12, 24–7, 29, 31, 33
chi-square tests 78, 79
citizens 37, 38, 45, 64, 65, 75, 86
Clark, Jennifer Hayes 38–40, 44
coding 27, 53, 57
conceptual groundwork 3, 14, 16
confirmatory factor analysis 68
Congress 37, 45, 46
congressional elections 45
control variables 78, 83
Conway, B. A. 50–1
covariates 68
cultural political brand perspective 11, 13

data analytic procedures 68
databases 6, 8
Debelko 39

Democratic candidates 41, 87
Democratic women 39, 42, 43, 45
Democrats 39–42, 66, 68, 75–9, 87–9
dependent variables 42, 70, 77
Dillard, James Price 67
direct effects 68
distinct brand perspectives 14, 15
Dolan, Kathleen 39

economy 29, 38, 40, 41, 45, 54, 56, 87, 88
election campaigns 75, 84
election day 24, 27, 28, 30, 31, 61, 77
election deniers 88, 89
election, 2022 87–8
employment 8, 54
Evans, Heather K. 38–40, 44

female candidates 2, 37–41, 43–6
Fishbein, Martin 67
foreign policy 54
freedom 62, 63, 65, 67, 70, 71
freedom threat 62, 63, 67–9, 71; and reactance 63, 68, 69
French, A. 15

gain-framed messages 63, 68, 69
Gainous, Jason 39
Gaver, W. W. 24
gender 2, 38–40, 42, 44, 45, 65, 66, 77, 78, 80; stereotypes 38
Gerber, Alan S. 64
Gerring, J. 16n3
Gibson, J. J. 24
government corruption 54, 56
Green, Donald P. 64

Harris, P. 15
Hayes, Danny 38–9
healthcare 29, 38–41, 54, 56
Herrick, Rebekah 39
Herrnson, Paul S. 39

92 INDEX

Holman, Mirya R. 39
Hurley, Z. 24

impeachment 56
individual voter 11, 13, 86
induction 67
Instagram 23–7, 29–31, 34, 76–80, 83
intermedia agenda-setting effects 49

Jensen, Jakob D. 63

Keane, Lauren Deschamps 64
Kenski, K. 50, 51
Klar, S. 76
Kline, RexB 68
Kreiss, D. 25, 26
Krosnick, Jon A. 63
Krupnikov, Y. 76

Lawless, Jennifer L. 38–9
Lawrence, R. G. 25, 26
Li, B. 25
Liebhart, K. 26
Lock, A. 15
loss-framed messages 2, 63, 69, 70

Macafee, T. 76
male candidates 37, 38, 40, 41, 44
McGrath, Mary C. 64
McGregor, S. C. 25, 26
McLaughlin, B. 76
message frame 62, 66–9
Miller, Joanne M, 63
minimal definition 3, 4, 8, 9, 14
mobilization campaigns 61, 64, 70
mobilization study 66–9
moderating variable 78
Muñoz, C. L. 27

Nashmi, E. A. 25–7, 32
Needham, C. 16n1
negative cognitions 67, 68
news media 50, 51, 56
news-media-to-twitter relationship 50
newspaper index 53, 54, 56
Nickerson, David W. 64
non-registered voters 65, 70, 71
nonpartisans 76, 78, 80, 84

O'Keefe, Daniel J. 63
O'Shaughnessy, N. 15
online campaigning 39, 44

Painter, D. 25–7, 32
Panagopoulos, Costas 63
participants 12, 65–8, 70, 71, 77
partisanship 2, 37–45, 76, 80

party brands 3, 8, 11, 14
party identification 2, 40, 75–80, 83
political affiliation 78
political behavior 64
political brands 3–6, 8, 9, 11–15; community
    perspective 11, 12; concept 3–5, 8, 9, 13; field
    10, 14, 15; literature 3, 5, 9, 15; personality
    perspective 11, 12; research 3, 5
political campaigning/campaigns 25, 26, 31, 50, 86
political candidates 30, 76, 88
political communication 25, 31, 46; research
    25, 38
political events 3
political marketers 12, 16, 24, 26, 70, 71
political messages 23, 26, 28, 29
political parties 11–13, 34, 62, 74–6, 78, 80, 88
political representations 9
political science 3, 6
political transactions 5
positive associations 68, 69, 83
presidential campaign 12, 23, 74
presidential candidate evaluations 2, 74
presidential elections 27, 64, 87
psychological reactance 62, 63, 65, 69; theory 61,
    62, 65, 69

Quick, Brian L. 67

race 2, 38, 40, 44–6, 52, 65, 66, 77, 80, 86, 87
reactance 2, 62–5, 67–9, 71
relational political brand perspective 11
Republican Party 56, 86–8
Republican women 39, 42, 43, 45
Republicans 39–45, 66, 75–9, 87, 88
Reynolds-Tylus, Tobias 67

Schaffner, Brian F. 39
Shane-Simpson, C. 24
Shen, Lijiang 67
Smith, G. 15, 16n1
Snapchat 25, 26, 76–80, 83
social media 23–6, 31, 33, 34, 38, 39, 49–51, 74, 75,
    77; platforms 24–6, 75
social norms 64, 65
Speed, R. 16n1
stickers 23, 24, 29, 31–4
structural models 68, 69
systematic review 3–5, 8–10, 14

technologies 23, 24
technology features 26, 27, 29–31, 33, 34
third-party candidates 40–2
Towner, T. L. 27
Trump, Donald 24, 29, 51, 54, 75, 77, 86, 88;
    campaigns 29–34; stories 29, 30, 32–4
tweets 30, 39–45, 49, 51–3, 56
Tweneboah-Koduah, E. Y. 14, 15

INDEX 93

Twitter 2, 24, 38–40, 49, 50, 54–7, 74–7, 79, 80, 87; index 52, 54, 56; sources 56

vote 2, 61, 62, 64–71
voter mobilization 62, 65, 69; study 65, 66
voter registration 61–71; context of 63, 65, 69; study 65, 66
voter-centric political brand perspective 12
voters 3–5, 9, 11–14, 25, 29, 33, 38, 61, 87, 88; endorsements 27, 30

Wagner, Kevin M. 39
Wang, D. 50, 51
Weeks, B. E. 76, 83
Wells, Chris 56
women 2, 37–46; campaign 37; issues 2, 37–46
work 24–7, 38–40, 44–6, 50, 57, 61

YouTube 76–80, 83